PENGUIN BOOKS — GREAT IDEAS

Some Anatomies of Melancholy

Robert Burton
1577–1640

Robert Burton

Some Anatomies of Melancholy

PENGUIN BOOKS — GREAT IDEAS

PENGUIN BOOKS

Published by the Penguin Group
Penguin Books Ltd, 80 Strand, London WC2R ORL, England
Penguin Group (USA) Inc., 375 Hudson Street, New York, New York 10014, USA
Penguin Group (Canada), 90 Eglinton Avenue East, Suite 700, Toronto, Ontario, Canada M4P 2Y3
(a division of Pearson Penguin Canada Inc.)
Penguin Ireland, 25 St Stephen's Green, Dublin 2, Ireland
(a division of Penguin Books Ltd)
Penguin Group (Australia), 250 Camberwell Road, Camberwell, Victoria 3124, Australia
(a division of Pearson Australia Group Pty Ltd)
Penguin Books India Pvt Ltd, 11 Community Centre, Panchsheel Park, New Delhi – 110 017, India
Penguin Group (NZ), 67 Apollo Drive, Rosedale, North Shore 0632, New Zealand
(a division of Pearson New Zealand Ltd)
Penguin Books (South Africa) (Pty) Ltd, 24 Sturdee Avenue, Rosebank, Johannesburg 2196, South Africa

Penguin Books Ltd, Registered Offices: 80 Strand, London WC2R ORL, England

www.penguin.com

The Anatomy of Melancholy first published 1621
This selection first published 2008

1

All rights reserved

Set by Rowland Phototypesetting Ltd, Bury St Edmunds, Suffolk
Printed in England by Clays Ltd, St Ives plc

978-0-141-03678-6

www.greenpenguin.co.uk

Penguin Books is committed to a sustainable future
for our business, our readers and our planet.
The book in your hands is made from paper
certified by the Forest Stewardship Council.

Contents

Of the Matter of Melancholy

Of the matter of melancholy, there is much question betwixt Avicenna and Galen, as you may read in Cardan's Contradictions, Valesius' Controversies, Montanus, Prosper Calenus, Capivaccius, Bright, Ficinus, that have written either whole tracts, or copiously of it in their several treatises of this subject. 'What this humour is, or whence it proceeds, how it is engendered in the body, neither Galen nor any old writer hath sufficiently discussed,' as Jacchinus thinks: the neoterics cannot agree. Montanus, in his Consultations, holds melancholy to be material or immaterial: and so doth Arculanus. The material is one of the four humours before mentioned, and natural; the immaterial or adventitious, acquisite, redundant, unnatural, artificial; which Hercules de Saxonia will have reside in the spirits alone, and to proceed from a 'hot, cold, dry, moist distemperature, which, without matter, alters the brain and functions of it.' Paracelsus wholly rejects and derides this division of four humours and complexions, but our Galenists generally approve of it, subscribing to this opinion of Montanus.

This material melancholy is either simple or mixed; offending in quantity or quality, varying according to his place, where it settleth, as brain, spleen, meseraic veins, heart, womb, and stomach; or differing according to the mixture of those natural humours amongst themselves, or four unnatural adust humours, as they are diversely tempered and mingled. If natural melancholy abound in the body, which is cold and dry, 'so that it be more than the body is well able to bear, it must needs be distempered,' saith Faventius, 'and diseased'; and so the other, if it be depraved, whether it arise from that other melancholy of choler adust, or from blood, produceth the like effects, and is, as Montaltus contends, if it come by adustion of humours, most part hot and dry. Some difference I find, whether this melancholy matter may be engendered of all four humours, about the colour and temper of it. Galen holds it may be engendered of three alone, excluding phlegm, or pituita, whose true assertion Valesius and Menardus stiffly maintain, and so doth Fuchsius, Montaltus, Montanus. How (say they) can white become black? But Hercules de Saxonia, *lib. post. de mela. cap.* 8, and Cardan are of the opposite part (it may be engendered of phlegm, *etsi raro contingat*, though it seldom come to pass); so is Guianerius, and Laurentius, *cap.* 1, with Melancthon in his book *de Anima*, and chap. of Humours; he calls it *asininam*, dull, swinish melancholy, and saith that he was an eye-witness of it: so is Wecker. From melancholy adust ariseth one kind; from choler another, which is most brutish; another from phlegm, which is dull; and the last from blood, which is best. Of these some are cold and dry, others hot and dry, varying according to their mixtures, as they are intended and remitted. And indeed, as Rodericus à Fons., *cons.* 12, *lib.* 1, determines, ichors and those serous matters being thickened become phlegm, and phlegm degenerates into choler, choler adust becomes *æruginosa melancholia* [rusty melancholy], as vinegar out of purest wine putrefied or by exhalation of purer spirits is so made, and becomes sour and sharp; and from the sharpness of this humour proceeds much waking, troublesome thoughts and dreams, etc., so that I conclude as before. If the humour be cold, it is, saith Faventinus, 'a cause of dotage, and produceth milder symptoms: if hot, they are rash, raving mad, or inclining to it.' If the brain be hot, the animal spirits are hot; much madness follows, with violent actions: if cold, fatuity and sottishness (Capivaccius). 'The colour of this mixture varies likewise according to the mixture, be it hot or cold; 'tis sometimes black, sometimes not' (Altomarus). The same Melanelius proves out of Galen; and Hippocrates in his book of Melancholy (if at least it be his), giving instance in a burning coal, 'which when it is hot, shines; when it is cold, looks black; and so doth the humour.' This diversity of melancholy matter produceth diversity of effects. If it be within the body, and not putrefied, it causeth black jaundice; if putrefied, a quartan ague; if it break out to the skin, leprosy; if to parts, several maladies, as scurvy, etc. If it trouble the mind, as it is diversely mixed, it produceth several kinds of madness and dotage: of which in their place.

Of the Species or Kinds of Melancholy

When the matter is diverse and confused, how should it otherwise be but that the species should be diverse and confused? Many new and old writers have spoken confusedly of it, confounding melancholy and madness, as Heurnius, Guianerius, Gordonius, Sallustius Salvianus, Jason Pratensis, Savonarola, that will have madness no other than melancholy in extent, differing (as I have said) in degrees. Some make two distinct species, as Ruffus Ephesius, an old writer, Constantinus Africanus, Aretæus, Aurelianus, Paulus Ægineta: others acknowledge a multitude of kinds, and leave them indefinite, as Aetius in his *Tetrabiblos*, Avicenna, *lib. 3, fen. 1, tract 4, cap. 18*; Arculanus, *cap. 16, in 9 Rhasis*; Montanus, *Med. part. 1*. 'If natural melancholy be adust, it maketh one kind; if blood, another; if choler, a third, differing from the first; and so many several opinions there are about the kinds, as there be men themselves.' Hercules de Saxonia sets down two kinds, 'material and immaterial; one from spirits alone, the other from humours and spirits.' Savonarola, *rub. 11, tract. 6, cap. 1, de ægritud. capitis*, will have the kinds to be infinite; one from the myrach, called *myrachialis* of the Arabians; another *stomachalis*, from the stomach; another from the liver, heart, womb, hemrods: 'one beginning, another consummate.' Melancthon seconds him: 'As the humour is

4

diversely adust and mixed, so are the species diverse'; but what these men speak of species I think ought to be understood of symptoms, and so doth Arculanus interpret himself: infinite species, *id est*, symptoms; and in that sense, as Jo. Gorrhæus acknowledgeth in his Medicinal Definitions, the species are infinite, but they may be reduced to three kinds by reason of their seat; head, body, and hypochondries. This threefold division is approved by Hippocrates in his book of Melancholy (if it be his, which some suspect), by Galen, *lib. 3 de loc. affectis, cap.* 6; by Alexander, *lib.* 1, *cap.* 16; Rhasis, *lib.* 1 *Continent., Tract.* 9, *lib.* 1, *cap.* 16; Avicenna, and most of our new writers. Th. Erastus makes two kinds; one perpetual, which is head-melancholy; the other interrupt, which comes and goes by fits, which he subdivides into the other two kinds, so that all comes to the same pass. Some again make four or five kinds, with Rodericus à Castro, *de morbis mulier. lib.* 2, *cap.* 3, and Lod. Mercatus, who in his second book *de mulier. affect. cap.* 4, will have that melancholy of nuns, widows, and more ancient maids to be a peculiar species of melancholy differing from the rest: some will reduce enthusiasts, ecstatical and demoniacal persons to this rank, adding love-melancholy to the first, and lycanthropia. The most received division is into three kinds. The first proceeds from the sole fault of the brain, and is called head-melancholy; the second sympathetically proceeds from the whole body, when the whole temperature is melancholy: the third ariseth from the bowels, liver, spleen, or membrane called mesenterium, named hypochondriacal or windy melancholy, which Laurentius subdivides into three parts, from those three members, hepatic, splenetic, meseraic. Love-melancholy, which Avicenna calls *ilishi*, and lycanthropia, which he calls *cucubuth*, are commonly included in head-melancholy; but of this last, which Gerardus de Solo calls amorous, and most knight-melancholy, with that of religious melancholy, *virginum et viduarum* [of maids and widows], maintained by Rod. à Castro and Mercatus, and the other kinds of love-melancholy, I will speak of apart by themselves in my third partition. The three precedent species are the subject of my present discourse, which I will anatomize and treat of through all their causes, symptoms, cures, together and apart; that every man that is in any measure affected with this malady may know how to examine it in himself, and apply remedies unto it.

It is a hard matter, I confess, to distinguish these three species one from the other, to express their several causes, symptoms, cures, being that they are so often confounded amongst themselves, having such affinity that they can scarce be discerned by the most accurate physicians, and so often intermixed with other diseases that the best experienced have been plunged. Montanus, *consil.* 26, names a patient that had this disease of melancholy and *caninus appetitus* both together; and, *consil.* 23, with vertigo; Julius Cæsar Claudinus with stone, gout, jaundice; Trincavellius with an ague, jaundice, *caninus appetitus*, etc. Paulus Regoline, a great doctor in his time, consulted in this case, was so confounded with a confusion of symptoms, that he knew not to what kind of melancholy to refer it. Trincavellius, Fallopius, and Francanzanus, famous doctors in Italy, all three conferred with about one party at the same time, gave three different opinions. And in another place, Trincavellius being demanded what he thought of a melancholy young man to whom he was sent for, ingenuously confessed that he was indeed melancholy, but he knew not to what kind to reduce it. In his seventeenth consultation there is the like disagreement about a melancholy monk. Those symptoms, which others ascribe to misaffected parts and humours, Herc. de Saxonia attributes wholly to distempered spirits, and those immaterial, as I have said. Sometimes they cannot well discern this disease from others. In Reinerus Solenander's Counsels, *sect.* 3, *consil.* 5, he and Dr Brande both agreed that the patient's disease was hypochondriacal melancholy. Dr Matholdus said it was asthma, and nothing else. Solenander and Guarionius, lately sent for to the melancholy Duke of Cleve, with others, could not define what species it was, or agree amongst themselves. The species are so confounded, as in Cæsar Claudinus his forty-fourth consultation for a Polonian count; in his judgment 'he laboured of head melancholy, and that which proceeds from the whole temperature, both at once.' I could give instance of some that have had all three kinds *semel et simul* [all together], and some successively. So that I conclude of our melancholy species, as many politicians do of their pure forms of commonwealths, monarchies, aristocracies, democracies, are most famous in contemplation, but in practice they are temperate and usually mixed (so Polybius informeth us), as the Lacedæmonian, the Roman of old, German now, and many others. What physicians say of distinct species in their books it much matters not, since that in their patients' bodies they are commonly mixed. In such obscurity, therefore, variety and confused mixture of symptoms, causes, how difficult a thing is it to treat of several kinds apart; to make any certainty or distinction among so many casualties, distractions, when seldom two men shall be like affected *per omnia* [in all respects]! 'Tis hard, I confess, yet nevertheless I will adventure through the midst of these perplexities, and, led by the clue or thread of the best writers, extricate myself out of a labyrinth of doubts and errors, and so proceed to the causes.

Causes of Melancholy – God a Cause

'It is in vain to speak of cures, or think of remedies, until such time as we have considered of the causes,' so Galen prescribes Glauco: and the common experience of others confirms that those cures must be imperfect, lame, and to no purpose, wherein the causes have not first been searched, as Prosper Calenius well observes in his tract *de atra bile* to Cardinal Cæsius. Insomuch that Fernelius puts 'a kind of necessity in the knowledge of the causes, and without which it is impossible to cure or prevent any manner of disease.' Empirics may ease, and sometimes help, but not thoroughly root out; *sublata causa tollitur effectus*, as the saying is, if the cause be removed, the effect is likewise vanquished. It is a most difficult thing (I confess) to be able to discern these causes whence they are, and in such variety to say what the beginning was. He is happy that can perform it aright. I will adventure to guess as near as I can, and rip them all up, from the first to the last, general and particular, to every species, that so they may the better be described.

General causes are either supernatural or natural. Supernatural are from God and His angels, or by God's permission from the devil and his ministers. That God Himself is a cause for the punishment of sin, and satisfaction of His justice, many examples and testimonies of holy Scriptures make evident unto us. Ps. cvii, 17: 'Foolish

9

men are plagued for their offence, and by reason of their wickedness.' Gehazi was strucken with leprosy (2 Reg. v, 27); Jehoram with dysentery and flux, and great diseases of the bowels (2 Chron. xxi, 15); David plagued for numbering his people (1 Chron. xxi); Sodom and Gomorrah swallowed up. And this disease is peculiarly specified (Ps. cvii, 12), 'He brought down their heart through heaviness'; (Deut. xxviii, 28), 'He struck them with madness, blindness, and astonishment of heart'; 'An evil spirit was sent by the Lord upon Saul, to vex him'; Nebuchadnezzar did eat grass like an ox, and his 'heart was made like the beasts of the field.' Heathen stories are full of such punishments. Lycurgus, because he cut down the vines in the country, was by Bacchus driven into madness: so was Pentheus and his mother Agave for neglecting their sacrifice. Censor Fulvius ran mad for untiling Juno's temple, to cover a new one of his own, which he had dedicated to Fortune, 'and was confounded to death with grief and sorrow of heart.' When Xerxes would have spoiled Apollo's temple at Delphi of those infinite riches it possessed, a terrible thunder came from heaven and struck four thousand men dead, the rest ran mad. A little after, the like happened to Brennus, lightning, thunder, earthquakes, upon such a sacrilegious occasion. If we may believe our pontifical writers, they will relate unto us many strange and prodigious punishments in this kind, inflicted by their saints. How Clodoveus, sometime King of France, the son of Dagobert, lost his wits for uncovering the body of St Denis; and how a sacrilegious Frenchman, that would have stolen a silver image of St John, at Birgburge, became frantic on a sudden, raging, and tyrannizing over his own flesh; of a Lord of Radnor, that coming from hunting late at night, put his dogs into St Avan's Church (Llan Avan they called it), and rising betimes next morning, as hunters use to do, found all his dogs mad, himself being suddenly strucken blind; of Tiridates, an Armenian king, for violating some holy nuns, that was punished in like sort, with loss of his wits. But poets and papists may go together for fabulous tales; let them free their own credits: howsoever they feign of their Nemesis, and of their saints, or by the devil's means may be deluded, we find it true that *ultor a tergo Deus*, 'He is God the avenger,' as David styles Him; and that it is our crying sins that pull this and many other maladies on our own heads; that He can by His angels, which are His ministers, strike and heal (saith Dionysius) whom He will; that He can plague us by His creatures, sun, moon, and stars, whom He useth as His instruments, as a husbandman (saith Zanchius) doth a hatchet: hail, snow, winds, etc. – *Et conjurati veniunt in classica venti* [the winds in a band answer His summons] – as in Joshua's time, as in Pharaoh's reign in Egypt, they are but as so many executioners of His justice. He can make the proudest spirits stoop, and cry out with Julian the Apostate, *Vicisti, Galilæe*; or with Apollo's priest in Chrysostom, *O cælum! O terra!* [O heaven! O earth!] *unde hostis hic?* what an enemy is this? and pray with David, acknowledging his power, 'I am weakened and sore broken, I roar for the grief of mine heart, mine heart panteth,' etc. (Ps. xxxviii, 8); 'O Lord, rebuke me not in thine anger, neither chastise me in thy wrath' (Ps. xxxviii, 1); 'Make me to hear joy and gladness, that the bones which thou hast broken may rejoice' (Ps. li, 8); 'Restore to me the joy of thy salvation, and stablish me with thy free spirit' (Ps. li, 12). For these causes belike Hippocrates would have a physician take special notice whether the disease come not from a divine supernatural cause, or whether it follow the course of nature. But this is further discussed by Fran. Valesius, *de sacr. philos. cap.* 8, Fernelius, and J. Cæsar Claudinus, to whom I refer you, how this place of Hippocrates is to be understood. Paracelsus is of opinion that such spiritual diseases (for so he calls them) are spiritually to be cured, and not otherwise. Ordinary means in such cases will not avail: *Non est reluctandum cum Deo* [we must not struggle with God]. When that monster-taming Hercules overcame all in the Olympics, Jupiter at last in an unknown shape wrestled with him; the victory was uncertain, till at length Jupiter descried himself, and Hercules yielded. No striving with supreme powers. *Nil uvat immensos Cratero promittere montes* [it avails not to promise Craterus gold mines for a cure], physicians and physic can do no good, 'we must submit ourselves unto the mighty hand of God, acknowledge our offences, call to Him for mercy.' If He strike us, *una eademque manus vulnus opemque feret* [the same hand will inflict the wound and provide the remedy], as it is with them that are wounded with the spear of Achilles, He alone must help; otherwise our diseases are incurable, and we not to be relieved.

A Digression of the Nature of Spirits, Bad Angels, or Devils, and how they cause Melancholy

How far the power of spirits and devils doth extend, and whether they can cause this, or any other disease, is a serious question, and worthy to be considered: for the better understanding of which, I will make a brief digression of the nature of spirits. And although the question be very obscure, according to Postellus, 'full of controversy and ambiguity,' beyond the reach of human capacity, *fateor excedere vires intentionis meæ*, saith Austin, I confess I am not able to understand it, *finitum de infinito non potest statuere* [the finite cannot decide about the infinite], we can sooner determine with Tully (*De nat. deorum*), *quid non sint, quam quid sint* [what they are not than what they are], our subtle schoolmen, Cardans, Scaligers, profound Thomists, *Fracastoriana et Ferneliana acies*, are weak, dry, obscure, defective in these mysteries, and all our quickest wits, as an owl's eyes at the sun's light, wax dull, and are not sufficient to apprehend them; yet, as in the rest, I will adventure to say something to this point. In former times, as we read (Acts xxiii), the Sadducees denied that there were any such spirits, devils, or angels. So did Galen the physician, the Peripatetics, even Aristotle himself, as Pomponatius stoutly maintains, and Scaliger in some sort grants, though Dandinus the Jesuit, *Com. in lib. 2 de anima*, stiffly denies it;

substantiæ separatæ [abstract substances] and intelligences
are the same which Christians call angels, and Platonists
devils, for they name all the spirits *dæmones*, be they
good or bad angels, as Julius Pollux, *Onomasticon, lib.* 1,
cap. 1, observes. Epicures and atheists are of the same
mind in general, because they never saw them. Plato,
Plotinus, Porphyrius, Iamblichus, Proclus, insisting in the
steps of Trismegistus, Pythagoras, and Socrates, make no
doubt of it: nor Stoics, but that there are such spirits,
though much erring from the truth. Concerning the first
beginning of them, the Talmudists say that Adam had
a wife called Lilis, before he married Eve, and of her
he begat nothing but devils. The Turks' Alcoran is
altogether as absurd and ridiculous in this point: but the
Scripture informs us Christians, how Lucifer, the chief
of them, with his associates, fell from heaven for his
pride and ambition; created of God, placed in heaven,
and sometime an angel of light, now cast down into the
lower aerial sublunary parts, or into hell, 'and delivered
into chains of darkness to be kept unto damnation' (2 Pet.
ii, 4). There is a foolish opinion which some hold, that
they are the souls of men departed; good and more noble
were deified, the baser grovelled on the ground, or
in the lower parts, and were devils; the which, with
Tertullian, Porphyrius the philosopher, M. Tyrius, *ser.* 27,
maintains. 'These spirits,' he saith, 'which we call angels
and devils, are naught but souls of men departed, which
either through love and pity of their friends yet living,
help and assist them, or else persecute their enemies,
whom they hated,' as Dido threatened to persecute
Æneas:

Omnibus umbra locis adero: dabis, improbe, pœnas.

[My angry ghost, arising from the deep,
Shall haunt thee waking, and disturb thy sleep.]

They are (as others suppose) appointed by those higher powers to keep men from their nativity, and to protect or punish them as they see cause: and are called *boni* and *mali genii* by the Romans; heroes, lares if good, lemures or larvæ if bad, by the Stoics; governors of countries, men, cities, saith Apuleius: *Deos appellant qui ex hominum numero juste ac prudenter vitæ curriculo gubernato, pro numine, postea ab hominibus præditi fanis et ceremoniis vulgo admittuntur, ut in Ægypto Osiris* [they call gods those who, having as men lived justly and wisely on earth, are after their death deified, and honoured with temples and rites, like Osiris in Egypt], etc. *Præstites* [protectors], Capella calls them, 'which protected particular men as well as princes.' Socrates had his *dæmonium saturninum et igneum* [saturnine and fiery familiar spirit], which of all spirits is best *ad sublimes cogitationes animum erigentem* [for stirring the mind to sublime reflections], as the Platonists supposed; Plotinus his; and we Christians our assisting angel, as Andreas Victorellus, a copious writer of this subject, Lodovicus de LaCerda, the Jesuit, in his voluminous tract *de Angelo Custode*, Zanchius, and some divines think. But this absurd tenent of Tyrius, Proclus confutes at large in his book *de anima et dæmone*.

Psellus, a Christian, and sometime tutor (saith Cuspinian) to Michael Parapinatius, Emperor of Greece, a great observer of the nature of devils, holds they are corporeal, and have 'aerial bodies, that they are mortal, live and die,' (which Martianus Capella likewise maintains, but our Christian philosophers explode), 'that they are nourished and have excrements, that they feel pain if they be hurt' (which Cardan confirms, and Scaliger justly laughs him to scorn for; *Si pascantur aere, cur non pugnant ob puriorem aera?* [If they feed on air, why do they not fight for purer air?], etc.) 'or stroken': and if their bodies be cut, with admirable celerity they come together again. Austin, *in Gen. lib. 3, lib. arbit.*, approves as much, *mutato casu corpora in deteriorem qualitatem aeris spissioris* [conversely, their bodies can be changed to an air of inferior and coarser quality]; so doth Hierome, *Comment. in Epist. ad Ephes. cap. 3*, Origen, Tertullian, Lactantius, and many ancient Fathers of the Church: that in their fall their bodies were changed into a more aerial and gross substance. Bodine, *lib. 4 Theatri Naturæ*, and David Crusius, *Hermeticæ Philosophiæ lib. 1, cap. 4*, by several arguments proves angels and spirits to be corporeal: *Quicquid continetur in loco corporeum est: At spiritus continetur in loco, ergo* [whatever occupies space is corporeal; spirit occupies space, therefore, etc.]. *Si spiritus sunt quanti, erunt corporei: At sunt quanti, ergo. Sunt finiti, ergo quanti* [If spirits are quantities, they must be corporeal; but they are quantities, therefore . . . They are finite, therefore quantitative], etc. Bodine goes farther yet, and will have these *animæ separatæ* [abstract souls], genii, spirits, angels, devils, and so likewise souls of men departed, if corporeal (which he most eagerly contends), to be of some shape, and that absolutely round, like sun and moon, because that is the most perfect form, *quæ nihil habet asperitatis, nihil angulis incisum, nihil anfractibus involutum, nihil eminens, sed inter corpora perfecta est perfectissimum* [which has no rough edges, no corners, no twists, no projections, but is the most perfect of shapes]; therefore all spirits are corporeal, he concludes, and in their proper shapes round. That they can assume other aerial bodies, all manner of shapes at their pleasures, appear in what likeness they will themselves, that they are most swift in motion, can pass many miles in an instant, and so likewise transform bodies of others into what shape they please, and with admirable celerity remove them from place to place (as the angel did Habakkuk to Daniel, and as Philip the Deacon was carried away by the Spirit, when he had baptized the eunuch; so did Pythagoras and Apollonius remove themselves and others, with many such feats); that they can represent castles in the air, palaces, armies, spectrums, prodigies, and such strange objects to mortal men's eyes, cause smells, savours, etc., deceive all the senses; most writers of this subject credibly believe; and that they can foretell future events, and do many strange miracles. Juno's image spake to Camillus, and Fortune's statue to the Roman matrons, with many such. Zanchius, Bodine, Spondanus, and others, are of opinion that they cause a true metamorphosis, as Nebuchadnezzar was really translated into a beast, Lot's wife into a pillar of salt, Ulysses' companions into hogs and dogs by Circe's charms; turn themselves and others, as they do witches, into cats, dogs, hares, crows, etc. Strozzius Cicogna hath many examples, *lib.* 3 *Omnif. mag. cap.* 4 *et* 5, which he there confutes, as Austin likewise doth, *de Civ. Dei, lib.* 18.

That they can be seen when, and in what shape, and to whom they will, saith Psellus, *tametsi nil tale viderim, nec optem videre*, though he himself never saw them nor desired it; and use sometimes carnal copulation (as elsewhere I shall prove more at large) with women and men. Many will not believe they can be seen, and if any man shall say, swear, and stiffly maintain, though he be discreet and wise, judicious and learned, that he hath seen them, they account him a timorous fool, a melancholy dizzard, a weak fellow, a dreamer, a sick or a mad man, they contemn him, laugh him to scorn, and yet Marcus of his credit told Psellus that he had often seen them. And Leo Suavius, a Frenchman, *cap.* 8, *in Commentar. lib.* i *Paracelsi de vita longa*, out of some Platonists, will have the air to be as full of them as snow falling in the skies, and that they may be seen, and withal sets down the means how men may see them: *Si irreverberatis oculis sole splendente versus cœlum continuaverint obtutus* [by looking steadfastly at the sky, in bright sunshine, without blinking], etc., and saith moreover he tried it, *præmissorum feci experimentum*, and it was true that the Platonists said. Paracelsus confesseth that he saw them divers times, and conferred with them, and so doth Alexander ab Alexandro, 'that he so found it by experience, whenas before he doubted of it.' Many deny it, saith Lavater, *de spectris, part.* i, *cap.* 2, and *part.* 2, *cap.* ii, 'because they never saw them themselves'; but as he reports at large all over his book, especially *cap.* 19, *part.* i, they are often seen and heard, and familiarly converse with men, as Lod. Vives assureth us, innumerable records, histories, and testimonies evince in all ages, times, places, and all travellers besides; in the West Indies and our northern climes, *nihil familiarius quam in agris et urbibus spiritus videre, audire qui vetent, jubeant* [nothing is more common than to see spirits both in town and country, and to hear them ordering or forbidding something], etc. Hieronymus, *vita Pauli*, Basil, *ser.* 40, Nicephorus, Eusebius, Socrates, Sozomenus, Jacobus Boissardus in his tract *de spirituum apparitionibus*, Petrus Loyerus, *lib. de spectris*, Wierus, *lib.* 1, have infinite variety of such examples of apparitions of spirits, for him to read that further doubts, to his ample satisfaction. One alone I will briefly insert. A nobleman in Germany was sent ambassador to the King of Sweden (for his name, the time, and such circumstances, I refer you to Boissardus, mine author). After he had done his business, he sailed to Livonia, on set purpose to see those familiar spirits, which are there said to be conversant with men and do their drudgery works. Amongst other matters, one of them told him where his wife was, in what room, in what clothes, what doing, and brought him a ring from her, which at his return, *non sine omnium admiratione* [to the general surprise], he found to be true; and so believed that ever after, which before he doubted of. Cardan, *lib.* 19 *de subtil.*, relates of his father, Facius Cardan, that after the accustomed solemnities, *ann.* 1491, 13 August, he conjured up seven devils in Greek apparel, about forty years of age, some ruddy of complexion, and some pale, as he thought; he asked them many questions, and they made ready answer, that they were aerial devils, that they lived and died as men did, save that they were far longer lived (seven or eight hundred years); they did as much excel men in dignity as we do juments, and were as far excelled again of those that were above them; our governors and keepers they are, moreover, which Plato in *Critias* delivered of old, and subordinate to one another, *ut enim homo homini, sic dæmon dæmoni dominatur* [for as man rules man, so devil rules devil], they rule themselves as well as us, and the spirits of the meaner sort had commonly such offices, as we make horsekeepers, neatherds, and the basest of us overseers of our cattle; and that we can no more apprehend their natures and functions than a horse a man's. They knew all things, but might not reveal them to men; and ruled and domineered over us, as we do over our horses; the best kings amongst us, and the most generous spirits, were not comparable to the basest of them. Sometimes they did instruct men, and communicate their skill, reward and cherish, and sometimes again terrify and punish, to keep them in awe, as they thought fit, *nihil magis cupientes* (saith Lysius, *Phys. Stoicorum*) *quam adorationem hominum* [longing for nothing more than the worship of mankind]. The same author, Cardan, in his *Hyperchen*, out of the doctrine of Stoics, will have some of these genii (for so he calls them) to be desirous of men's company, very affable and familiar with them, as dogs are; others, again, to abhor as serpents, and care not for them. The same, belike, Trithemius calls *igneos et sublunares, qui nunquam demergunt ad inferiora, aut vix ullum habent in terris commercium* [fiery and sublunar, who never descend to the lower sphere, and have little to do with the earth]. 'Generally they far excel men in worth, as a man the meanest worm; though some of them are inferior to those of their own rank in worth as the black guard in a prince's court, and to men again as some degenerate, base, rational creatures are excelled of brute beasts.'

That they are mortal, besides these testimonies of Cardan, Martianus, etc., many other divines and philosophers hold, *post prolixum tempus moriuntur omnes* [they all die after a great lapse of time]; the Platonists and some Rabbins, Porphyrius, and Plutarch, as appears by that relation of Thamus: 'The great God Pan is dead'; Apollo Pythius ceased; and so the rest. St Hierome, in the life of Paul the Eremite, tells a story how one of them appeared to St Anthony in the wilderness, and told him as much. Paracelsus, of our late writers, stiffly maintains that they are mortal, live and die as other creatures do. Zozimus, *lib.* 2, farther adds, that religion and policy dies and alters with them. The Gentiles' gods, he saith, were expelled by Constantine, and together with them *imperii Romani majestas et fortuna interiit, et profligata est*, the fortune and majesty of the Roman Empire decayed and vanished; as that heathen in Minucius formerly bragged, when the Jews were overcome by the Romans, the Jews' God was likewise captivated by that of Rome; and Rabshakeh to the Israelites, no God should deliver them out of the hands of the Assyrians. But these paradoxes of their power, corporeity, mortality, taking of shapes, transposing bodies, and carnal copulations, are sufficiently confuted by Zanch. *cap.* 10, *lib.* 4; Pererius, in his Comment, and Tostatus' questions on the 6th of Gen.; Th. Aquin., St Austin, Wierus, Th. Erastus, Delrio, *tom.* 2, *lib.* 2, *quæst.* 29; Sebastian Michaelis, *cap.* 2 *de spiritibus*, Dr Rainolds, *Lect.* 47. They may deceive the

eyes of men, yet not take true bodies, or make a real
metamorphosis; but as Cicogna proves at large, they are
*illusoriæ et præstigiatrices transformationes (Omnif. mag. lib.
4, cap.* 4), mere illusions and cozenings, like that tale of
Pasetis obolus in Suidas, or that of Autolycus, Mercury's
son that dwelt in Parnassus, who got so much treasure
by cozenage and stealth. His father Mercury, because he
could leave him no wealth, taught him many fine tricks
to get means, for he could drive away men's cattle, and
if any pursued him, turn them into what shapes he
would, and so did mightily enrich himself, *hoc astu
maximam prædam est adsecutus.* This, no doubt, is as true
as the rest; yet thus much in general Thomas, Durand,
and others grant, that they have understanding far
beyond men, can probably conjecture and foretell many
things; they can cause and cure most diseases, deceive
our senses; they have excellent skill in all arts and sciences; and that the most illiterate devil is *quovis homine
scientior* (more knowing than any man), as Cicogna maintains out of others. They know the virtues of herbs,
plants, stones, minerals, etc., of all creatures, birds,
beasts, the four elements, stars, planets; can aptly apply
and make use of them as they see good; perceiving the
causes of all meteors, and the like. *Dant se coloribus* (as
Austin hath it), *accommodant se figuris, adhærent sonis,
subjiciunt se odoribus, infundunt se saporibus* [they insert
themselves into colours, shapes, sounds, smells, and
tastes], *omnes sensus etiam ipsam intelligentiam dæmones
fallunt,* they deceive all our senses, even our understanding itself at once. They can produce miraculous alter-
ations in the air, and most wonderful effects, conquer

armies, give victories, help, further, hurt, cross, and alter human attempts and projects (*Dei permissu*) as they see good themselves. When Charles the Great intended to make a channel betwixt the Rhine and Danubius, look what his workmen did in the day, these spirits flung down in the night, *ut conatu rex desisteret, pervicere* [they succeeded in making the king desist from his attempt]. Such feats can they do. But that which Bodine, *lib. 4 Theat. nat.*, thinks (following Tyrius belike, and the Platonists), they can tell the secrets of a man's heart, *aut cogitationes hominum*, is most false; his reasons are weak, and sufficiently confuted by Zanch., *lib. 4, cap. 9*; Hierome, *lib. 2 Com. in Mat. ad cap. 15*, Athanasius, *Quæst. 27 ad Antiochum Principem*, and others.

As for those orders of good and bad devils, [that] which the Platonists hold is altogether erroneous, and those ethnics' *boni* and *mali genii* [good and bad genii] are to be exploded: these heathen writers agree not in this point among themselves, as Dandinus notes, *An sint mali non conveniunt* [they are not agreed as to whether there are any bad]; some will have all spirits good or bad to us by a mistake; as if an ox or horse could discourse, he would say the butcher was his enemy because he killed him, the grazier his friend because he fed him; an hunter preserves and yet kills his game, and is hated nevertheless of his game; *nec piscatorem piscis amare potest* [the fish cannot love the fisherman], etc. But Iamblichus, Psellus, Plutarch, and most Platonists acknowledge bad, *et ab eorum maleficiis cavendum* [and we should beware of their wickedness], for they are enemies of mankind, and this Plato learned in Egypt, that they quarrelled with

Jupiter, and were driven by him down to hell. That which Apuleius, Xenophon, and Plato contend of Socrates' *dæmonium*, is most absurd: that which Plotinus of his, that he had likewise *deum pro dæmonio* [a god for his familiar spirit]; and that which Porphyry concludes of them all in general, if they be neglected in their sacrifice they are angry; nay more, as Cardan in his *Hyperchen* will, they feed on men's souls: *Elementa sunt plantis elementum, animalibus plantæ, hominibus animalia, erunt et homines aliis, non autem diis, nimis enim remota est eorum natura a nostra, quapropter dæmonibus* [minerals are food for plants, plants for animals, animals for men; men will also be food for other creatures, but not for gods, for their nature is far removed from ours; it must therefore be for devils]; and so, belike, that we have so many battles fought in all ages, countries, is to make them a feast, and their sole delight: but to return to that I said before, if displeased they fret and chafe (for they feed, belike, on the souls of beasts, as we do on their bodies), and send many plagues amongst us; but if pleased, then they do much good; is as vain as the rest, and confuted by Austin, *lib.* 9, *cap.* 8, *de Civ. Dei.*, Euseb., *lib.* 4 *Præpar. Evang. cap.* 6, and others. Yet thus much I find, that our schoolmen and other divines make nine kinds of bad spirits, as Dionysius hath done of angels. In the first rank are those false gods of the Gentiles, which were adored heretofore in several idols, and gave oracles at Delphi, and elsewhere; whose prince is Beelzebub. The second rank is of liars and equivocators, as Apollo Pythius and the like. The third are those vessels of anger, inventors of all mischief; as that Theuth in Plato; Esay calls them vessels of fury; their prince is Belial. The fourth are malicious revenging devils; and their prince is Asmodæus. The fifth kind are cozeners, such as belong to magicians and witches; their prince is Satan. The sixth are those aerial devils that corrupt the air and cause plagues, thunders, fires, etc.; spoken of in the Apocalypse, and Paul to the Ephesians names them the princes of the air; Meresin is their prince. The seventh is a destroyer, captain of the Furies, causing wars, tumults, combustions, uproars, mentioned in the Apocalypse, and called Abaddon. The eighth is that accusing or calumniating devil, whom the Greeks call Διάβολος, that drives men to despair. The ninth are those tempters in several kinds, and their prince is Mammon. Psellus makes six kinds, yet none above the moon; Wierus, in his *Pseudomonarchia Dæmonis*, out of an old book, makes many more divisions and subordinations, with their several names, numbers, offices, etc., but Gazæus, cited by Lipsius, will have all places full of angels, spirits, and devils, above and beneath the moon, ætherial and aerial, which Austin cites out of Varro, *lib.* 7 *de Civ. Dei*, *cap.* 6, 'the celestial devils above, and aerial beneath,' or, as some will, gods above, *semidei* or half-gods beneath, lares, heroes, genii, which climb higher, if they lived well, as the Stoics held, but grovel on the ground as they were baser in their lives, nearer to the earth: and are manes, lemures, lamiæ, etc. They will have no place void, but all full of spirits, devils, or some other inhabitants; *plenum cœlum, aer, aqua, terra, et omnia sub terra* [full is the sky, the air, the sea, the earth, and all beneath the earth], saith Gazæus; though Anthony Rusca, in his book *de Inferno*, *lib.* 5, *cap.* 7, would confine them to the middle region, yet they will have them everywhere, 'not so much as an hairbreadth empty in heaven, earth, or waters, above or under the earth.' The air is not so full of flies in summer as it is at all times of invisible devils: this Paracelsus stiffly maintains, and that they have every one their several chaos; others will have infinite worlds, and each world his peculiar spirits, gods, angels, and devils to govern and punish it.

> *Singula nonnulli credunt quoque sidera posse*
> *Dici orbes, terramque appellant sidus opacum,*
> *Cui minimus divum præsit.*

[Some, too, believe that each star may also be called a world, and regard this earth as a dark star over which the least of the gods presides.]

Gregorius Tholosanus makes seven kinds of ætherial spirits or angels, according to the number of the seven planets, Saturnine, Jovial, Martial, of which Cardan discourseth, *lib.* 20 *de subtil.*; he calls them *substantias primas* [primary substances]; *Olympicos dæmones Trithemius, qui præsunt zodiaco* [Trithemius calls them Olympian spirits which rule the zodiac], etc., and will have them to be good angels above, devils beneath the moon; their several names and offices he there sets down, and, which Dionysius of angels, will have several spirits for several countries, men, offices, etc., which live about them, and as so many assisting powers cause their operations; will have, in a word, innumerable, as many of them as there be stars in the skies. Marsilius Ficinus seems to second this opinion, out of Plato, or from himself, I know not (still ruling their inferiors, as they do those under them again, all subordinate, and the nearest to the earth rule us, whom we subdivide into good and bad angels, call gods or devils, as they help or hurt us, and so adore, love or hate), but it is most likely from Plato, for he, relying wholly on Socrates, *quem mori potius quam mentiri voluisse scribit* [who, he says, would rather die than tell a false-hood], out of Socrates' authority alone, made nine kinds of them; which opinion, belike, Socrates took from Pythagoras, and he from Trismegistus, he from Zoro-aster: 1, God; 2, Ideæ; 3, Intelligences; 4, Archangels; 5, Angels; 6, Devils; 7, Heroes; 8, Principalities; 9, Princes: of which some were absolutely good, as gods, some bad, some indifferent *inter deos et homines* [between gods and men], as heroes and dæmons, which ruled men, and were called genii, or as Proclus and Iamblichus will, the middle betwixt God and men, principalities and princes, which commanded and swayed kings and countries, and had several places in the spheres perhaps, for as every sphere is higher, so hath it more excellent inhabitants: which, belike, is that Galilæus à Galilæo and Kepler aims at in his *Nuncio Sidereo*, when he will have Saturnine and Jovial inhabitants: and which Tycho Brahe doth in some sort touch or insinuate in one of his epistles: but these things Zanchius justly explodes, *cap.* 3, *lib.* 4; P. Martyr *in* 1 *Sam.* 28.

So that according to these men the number of ætherial spirits must needs be infinite; for if that be true that some of our mathematicians say: if a stone could fall from the starry heaven, or eighth sphere, and should pass every hour an hundred miles, it would be 65 years, or more, before it would come to ground, by reason of the great distance of heaven from earth, which contains, as some say, 170 millions 803 miles, besides those other heavens, whether they be crystalline or watery, which Maginus adds, which peradventure holds as much more; how many such spirits may it contain? And yet for all this Thomas, Albertus, and most, hold that there be far more angels than devils.

But be they more or less, *Quod supra nos nihil ad nos* [what is beyond our comprehension does not concern us]. Howsoever, as Martianus foolishly supposeth, *Ætherii dæmones non curant res humanas*, they care not for us, do not attend our actions, or look for us, those ætherial spirits have other worlds to reign in, belike, or business to follow. We are only now to speak in brief of those sublunary spirits or devils: for the rest, our divines determine that the devil had no power over stars or heavens. *Carminibus cœlo possunt deducere lunam* [by their charms (verses) they can seduce the moon from the heavens], etc. – those are poetical fictions; and that they can *sistere aquam fluviis, et vertere sidera retro* [stop rivers and turn the stars backward in their courses], etc., as Canidia in Horace, 'tis all false. They are confined until the day of judgment to this sublunary world, and can work no farther than the four elements, and as God permits them. Wherefore of these sublunary devils, though others divide them otherwise according to their several places and offices, Psellus makes six kinds, fiery, aerial, terrestrial, watery, and subterranean devils, besides those fairies, satyrs, nymphs, etc.

Fiery spirits or devils are such as commonly work by blazing stars, fire-drakes, or *ignes fatui*; which lead men often *in flumina aut præcipitia* [into rivers or over precipices], saith Bodine, *lib. 2 Theat. naturæ, fol.* 221. *Quos, inquit, arcere si volunt viatores, clara voce Deum appellare aut prona facie terram contingente adorare oportet, et hoc amuletum majoribus nostris acceptum ferre debemus* [whom if travellers wish to keep off they must pronounce the name of God with a clear voice, or adore Him with their faces in contact with the ground], etc.; likewise they counterfeit suns and moons, stars oftentimes, and sit on ship-masts: *in navigiorum summitatibus visuntur*; and are called *Dioscuri*, as Eusebius, *lib. contra Philosophos, cap.* 48, informeth us, out of the authority of Zenophanes; or little clouds, *ad motum nescio quem volantes* [scudding along all ways]; which never appear, saith Cardan, but they signify some mischief or other to come unto men, though some again will have them to pretend good, and victory to that side they come towards in sea fights; St Elmo's fires they commonly call them, and they do likely appear after a sea storm; Radzivilius, the Polonian duke, calls this apparition *Sancti Germani sidus* [the star of St Germanus]; and saith moreover that he saw the same after or in a storm, as he was sailing, 1582, from Alexandria to Rhodes. Our stories are full of such apparitions in all kinds. Some think they keep their residence in that Hecla, a mountain in Iceland, Ætna in Sicily, Lipari, Vesuvius, etc. These devils were worshipped heretofore by that superstitious Πυρομαντεία [divination by fire] and the like.

Aerial spirits or devils are such as keep quarter most

part in the air, cause many tempests, thunder, and lightnings, tear oaks, fire steeples, houses, strike men and beasts, make it rain stones, as in Livy's time, wool, frogs, etc., counterfeit armies in the air, strange noises, swords, etc., as at Vienna before the coming of the Turks, and many times in Rome, as Scheretzius, *lib. de spect. cap.* 1, *part.* 1; Lavater, *de spect. part.* 1, *cap.* 17; Julius Obsequens, an old Roman, in his book of prodigies, *ab urb. cond.* 505. Machiavel hath illustrated by many examples, and Josephus, in his book *de bello Judaico*, before the destruction of Jerusalem. All which Guil. Postellus, in his first book, *cap.* 7, *de orbis concordia*, useth as an effectual argument (as indeed it is) to persuade them that will not believe there be spirits or devils. They cause whirlwinds on a sudden, and tempestuous storms; which though our meteorologists generally refer to natural causes, yet I am of Bodine's mind, *Theat. Nat. lib.* 2, they are more often caused by those aerial devils, in their several quarters; for *tempestatibus se ingerunt* [they ride on the storm], saith Rich. Argentine; as when a desperate man makes away himself, which by hanging or drowning they frequently do, as Kornmannus observes, *de mirac. mort. part.* 7, *cap.* 76, *tripudium agentes*, dancing and rejoicing at the death of a sinner. These can corrupt the air, and cause plagues, sickness, storms, shipwrecks, fires, inundations. At Mons Draconis in Italy, there is a most memorable example in Jovianus Pontanus: and nothing so familiar (if we may believe those relations of Saxo Grammaticus, Olaus Magnus, Damianus à Goes) as for witches and sorcerers, in Lapland, Lithuania, and all over Scandia, to sell winds to mariners, and cause tempests, which Marcus Paulus the Venetian relates likewise of the Tartars. These kind of devils are much delighted in sacrifices (saith Porphyry), held all the world in awe, and had several names, idols, sacrifices, in Rome, Greece, Egypt, and at this day tyrannize over and deceive those ethnics and Indians, being adored and worshipped for gods. For the Gentiles' gods were devils (as Trismegistus confesseth in his *Asclepius*), and he himself could make them come to their images by magic spells: and are now as much 'respected by our papists' (saith Pictorius) 'under the name of saints.' These are they which Cardan thinks desire so much carnal copulation with witches (incubi and succubi), transform bodies, and are so very cold if they be touched; and that serve magicians. His father had one of them (as he is not ashamed to relate), an aerial devil, bound to him for twenty and eight years. As Agrippa's dog had a devil tied to his collar; some think that Paracelsus (or else Erastus belies him) had one confined to his sword pummel; others wear them in rings, etc. Jannes and Jambres did many things of old by their help; Simon Magus, Cinops, Apollonius Tyanæus, Iamblichus, and Trithemius of late, that showed Maximilian the emperor his wife, after she was dead; *et verrucam in collo ejus* (saith Godelman) so much as the wart on her neck. Delrio, *lib.* 2, hath divers examples of their feats; Cicogna, *lib.* 3, *cap.* 3, and Wierus in his book *de præstig. dæmonum*; Boissardus, *de magis et veneficis*.

Water-devils are those naiades or water-nymphs which have been heretofore conversant about waters and rivers. The water (as Paracelsus thinks) is their chaos, wherein they live; some call them fairies, and say that Habundia is their queen; these cause inundations, many times shipwrecks, and deceive men divers ways, as succubæ, or otherwise, appearing most part (saith Trithemius) in women's shapes. Paracelsus hath several stories of them that have lived and been married to mortal men, and so continued for certain years with them, and after, upon some dislike, have forsaken them. Such a one was Egeria, with whom Numa was so familiar, Diana, Ceres, etc. Olaus Magnus hath a long narration of one Hotherus, a king of Sweden, that having lost his company, as he was hunting one day, met with these water-nymphs or fairies, and was feasted by them; and Hector Boethius, of Macbeth and Banquo, two Scottish lords, that, as they were wandering in the woods, had their fortunes told them by three strange women. To these, heretofore, they did use to sacrifice, by that ὑδρομαντεία or divination by waters.

Terrestrial devils are those lares, genii, fauns, satyrs, wood-nymphs, foliots, fairies, Robin Goodfellows, *trolli* [trolls], etc., which as they are most conversant with men, so they do them most harm. Some think it was they alone that kept the heathen people in awe of old, and had so many idols and temples erected to them. Of this range was Dagon amongst the Philistines, Bel amongst the Babylonians, Astarte amongst the Sidonians, Baal amongst the Samaritans, Isis and Osiris amongst the Egyptians, etc.; some put our fairies into this rank, which have been in former times adored with much superstition, with sweeping their houses, and setting of a pail of clean water, good victuals, and the like, and then they should not be pinched, but find money in their shoes, and be fortunate in their enterprises. These are they that dance on heaths and greens, as Lavater thinks with Trithemius, and, as Olaus Magnus adds, leave that green circle, which we commonly find in plain fields, which others hold to proceed from a meteor falling, or some accidental rankness of the ground, so Nature sports herself; they are sometimes seen by old women and children. Hieronym. Pauli, in his description of the city of Barcino in Spain, relates how they have been familiarly seen near that town, about fountains and hills. *Nonnunquam* (saith Trithemius) *in sua latibula montium simpliciores homines ducunt, stupenda mirantibus ostendentes miracula, nolarum sonitus, spectacula,* [sometimes they lead simple-minded peasants into their hiding-places in the mountains, where they show them marvellous sights, make them hear bells, and astonish them in other ways], etc. Giraldus Cambrensis gives instance in a monk of Wales that was so deluded. Paracelsus reckons up many places in Germany, where they do usually walk in little coats, some two foot long. A bigger kind there is of them called with us hobgoblins, and Robin Goodfellows, that would in those superstitious times grind corn for a mess of milk, cut wood, or do any manner of drudgery work. They would mend old irons in those Æolian isles of Lipari, in former ages, and have been often seen and heard. Tholosanus calls them *trollos* and *getulos*, and saith that in his days they were common in many places of France. Dithmarus Bleskenius, in his description of Iceland, reports for a certainty, that almost in every family they have yet some such familiar spirits; and Felix Malleolus, in his book *de crudel. dæmon.*, affirms as much, that these *trolli* or *telchines* are very common in Norway, 'and seen to do drudgery work'; to draw water, saith Wierus, *lib.* 1, *cap.* 22, dress meat, or any such thing. Another sort of these there are, which frequent forlorn houses, which the Italians call foliots, most part innoxious, Cardan holds: 'They will make strange noises in the night, howl sometimes pitifully, and then laugh again, cause great flame and sudden lights, fling stones, rattle chains, shave men, open doors and shut them, fling down platters, stools, chests, sometimes appear in the likeness of hares, crows, black dogs, etc.,' of which read Pet. Thyræus the Jesuit, in his tract *de locis infestis, part.* 1, *cap.* 1 *et cap.* 4, who will have them to be devils or the souls of damned men that seek revenge, or else souls out of purgatory that seek ease; for such examples peruse Sigismundus Scheretzius, *lib. de spectris, part.* 1, *cap.* 1, which he saith he took out of Luther most part; there be many instances. Plinius Secundus remembers such a house at Athens, which Athenodorus the philosopher hired, which no man durst inhabit for fear of devils. Austin, *de Civ. Dei, lib.* 22, *cap.* 8, relates as much of Hesperius the tribune's house at Zubeda, near their city of Hippo, vexed with evil spirits, to his great hindrance, *cum afflictione animalium et servorum suorum* [and to the great distress of his animals and slaves]. Many such instances are to be read in Niderius, *Formicar. lib.* 5, *cap.* 12, 13, etc. Whether I may call these Zim and Ochim, which Isaiah, chap. xiii, 21, speaks of, I make a doubt. See more of these in the said Scheretz., *lib.* 1 *de spect. cap.* 4; he is full of examples. These kind of devils many times appear to men, and affright them out of their wits, sometimes walking at noonday, sometimes at nights, counterfeiting dead men's ghosts, as that of Caligula, which (saith Suetonius) was seen to walk in Lavinia's garden; where his body was buried, spirits haunted, and [in] the house where he died; *nulla nox sine terrore transacta, donec incendio consumpta*; every night this happened, there was no quietness till the house was burned. About Hecla, in Iceland, ghosts commonly walk, *animas mortuorum simulantes* [resembling the dead], saith Joh. Anan., *lib. 3 de nat. dæm.*, Olaus, *lib. 2, cap. 2,* Natal. Tallopid., *lib. de apparit. spir.*, Kornmannus, *de mirac. mort. part. 1, cap. 44*. Such sights are frequently seen *circa sepulchra et monasteria*, saith Lavater, *lib. 1, cap. 19*, in monasteries and about churchyards, *loca paludinosa, ampla ædificia, solitaria, et cæde hominum notata*, [marshes, great buildings, solitary places, or places remarkable as the scene of some murder] etc. Thyræus adds, *ubi gravius peccatum est commissum, impii pauperum oppressores et nequiter insignes habitant* [where some very heinous crime was committed, there the impious and infamous generally dwell]. These spirits often foretell men's deaths by several signs, as knocking, groanings, etc., though Rich. Argentine, *cap. 18 de præstigiis dæmonum*, will ascribe these predictions to good angels, out of the authority of Ficinus and others; *prodigia in obitu principum sæpius contingunt* [prodigies frequently occur at the deaths of illustrious men], etc., as in the Lateran Church in Rome, the Popes' deaths are foretold by Sylvester's tomb. Near Rupes Nova in Finland, in the kingdom of Sweden, there is a lake, in which, before the governor of the castle dies, a spectrum, in the habit of Arion with his harp, appears and makes excellent music; like those blocks in Cheshire, which (they say) presage death to the master of the family; or that oak in Lanthadran Park in Cornwall, which foreshows as much. Many families in Europe are so put in mind of their last by such predictions, and many men are forewarned (if we may believe Paracelsus) by familiar spirits in divers shapes, as cocks, crows, owls, which often hover about sick men's chambers, *vel quia morientium fœditatem sentiunt* [either because they smell a corpse], as Baracellus conjectures, *et ideo super tectum infirmorum crocitant* [and therefore they croak over a house where someone is lying ill], because they smell a corse; or for that (as Bernardinus de Bustis thinketh) God permits the devil to appear in the form of crows and such-like creatures, to scare such as live wickedly here on earth. A little before Tully's death (saith Plutarch) the crows made a mighty noise about him, *tumultuose perstrepentes*, they pulled the pillow from under his head. Rob. Gaguinus, *Hist. Franc. lib.* 8, telleth such another wonderful story at the death of Johannes de Monteforti, a French lord, *anno* 1345; *tanta corvorum multitudo ædibus morientis insedit, quantam esse in Gallia nemo judicasset* [a multitude of crows alighted on the house of the dying man, such as no one imagined existed in France]. Such prodigies are very frequent in authors. See more of these in the said Lavater, Thyræus, *de locis infestis, part.* 3, *cap.* 58, Pictorius, Delrio, Cicogna, *lib.* 3, *cap.* 9. Necromancers take upon them to raise and lay them at their pleasures. And so likewise those which Mizaldus calls *ambulones*, that walk about midnight on great heaths and desert places, which (saith Lavater) 'draw men out of the way, and lead them all night a by-way, or quite bar them of their way"; these have several names in several places; we commonly call them Pucks. In the deserts of Lop, in Asia, such illusions of walking spirits are often perceived, as you may read in M. Paulus the Venetian, his travels; if one lose his company by chance, these devils will call him by his name, and counterfeit voices of his companions to seduce him. Hieronym. Pauli, in his book of the hills of Spain, relates of a great mount in Cantabria, where such spectrums are to be seen; Lavater and Cicogna have variety of examples of spirits and walking devils in this kind. Sometimes they sit by the highway side, to give men falls, and make their horses stumble and start as they ride (if you will believe the relation of that holy man Ketellus in Nubrigensis, that had an especial grace to see devils, *gratiam divinitus collatam*, and talk with them, *et impavidus cum spiritibus sermonem miscere*, without offence); and if a man curse or spur his horse for stumbling they do heartily rejoice at it; with many such pretty feats.

Subterranean devils are as common as the rest, and do as much harm. Olaus Magnus, *lib. 6, cap.* 19, makes six kinds of them; some bigger, some less. These (saith Munster) are commonly seen about mines of metals, and are some of them noxious; some again do no harm. The metal-men in many places account it good luck, a sign of treasure and rich ore when they see them. Georgius Agricola, in his book *de subterraneis animantibus, cap.* 37, reckons two more notable kinds of them, which he calls *getuli* and *cobali*; both 'are clothed after the manner of metal-men, and will many times imitate their works.' Their office, as Pictorius and Paracelsus think, is to keep treasure in the earth, that it be not all at once revealed; and besides, Cicogna avers that they are the frequent causes of those horrible earthquakes 'which often swallow up, not only houses, but whole islands and cities'; in his third book, *cap.* 11, he gives many instances.

The last are conversant about the centre of the earth, to torture the souls of damned men to the day of judgment; their egress and regress some suppose to be about Ætna, Lipari, Mons Hecla in Iceland, Vesuvius, Terra del Fuego, etc., because many shrieks and fearful cries are continually heard thereabouts, and familiar apparitions of dead men, ghosts, and goblins.

Thus the devil reigns, and in a thousand several shapes, 'as a roaring lion still seeks whom he may devour' (1 Pet. v), by earth, sea, land, air, as yet unconfined, though some will have his proper place the air; all that space between us and the moon for them that transgressed least, and hell for the wickedest of them; *Hic velut in carcere ad finem mundi, tunc in locum funestiorum trudendi* [here they are confined as in a prison till the end of the world; then they are to be thrust forth into a still more dreadful place], as Austin holds, *de Civit. Dei, cap.* 22, *lib.* 14, *cap.* 3 *et* 23; but be where he will, he rageth while he may to comfort himself, as Lactantius thinks, with other men's falls, he labours all he can to bring them into the same pit of perdition with him. For 'men's miseries, calamities, and ruins are the devil's banqueting dishes.' By many temptations and several engines, he seeks to captivate our souls. The Lord of Lies, saith

Austin, 'as he was deceived himself, he seeks to deceive others'; the ringleader to all naughtiness, as he did by Eve and Cain, Sodom and Gomorrah, so would he do by all the world. Sometimes he tempts by covetousness, drunkenness, pleasure, pride, etc., errs, dejects, saves, kills, protects, and rides some men as they do their horses. He studies our overthrow, and generally seeks our destruction; and although he pretend many times human good, and vindicate himself for a god by curing of several diseases, *ægris sanitatem, et cæcis luminis usum restituendo* [by restoring health to the sick and sight to the blind] as Austin declares, *lib.* 10 *de Civit. Dei, cap.* 6, as Apollo, Æsculapius, Isis, of old have done; divert plagues, assist them in wars, pretend their happiness, yet *nihil his impurius, scelestius, nihil humano generi infestius,* nothing so impure, nothing so pernicious, as may well appear by their tyrannical and bloody sacrifices of men to Saturn and Moloch, which are still in use among those barbarous Indians, their several deceits and cozenings to keep men in obedience, their false oracles, sacrifices, their superstitious impositions of fasts, penury, etc., heresies, superstitious observations of meats, times, etc., by which they crucify the souls of mortal men, as shall be showed in our Treatise of Religious Melancholy. *Modico adhuc tempore sinitur malignari,* as Bernard expresseth it, by God's permission he rageth awhile, hereafter to be confined to hell and darkness, 'which is prepared for him and his angels' (Matt. xxv).

How far their power doth extend it is hard to determine; what the ancients held of their effects, force, and operations I will briefly show you. Plato in *Critias*, and after him his followers, gave out that these spirits or devils 'were men's governors and keepers, our lords and masters, as we are of our cattle. They govern provinces and kingdoms by oracles, auguries, dreams, rewards and punishments,' prophecies, inspirations, sacrifices, and religious superstitions, varied in as many forms as there be diversity of spirits; they send wars, plagues, peace, sickness, health, dearth, plenty, *adstantes hic jam nobis, spectantes, et arbitrantes* [standing by us here and now, watching and judging us], etc., as appears by those histories of Thucydides, Livius, Dionysius Halicarnasseus, with many others that are full of their wonderful stratagems, and were therefore by those Roman and Greek commonwealths adored and worshipped for gods with prayers and sacrifices, etc. In a word, *nihil magis quærunt quam metum et admirationem hominum* [they seek nothing more eagerly than the fear and admiration of men]; and as another hath it, *dici non potest, quam impotenti ardore in homines dominium, et divinos cultus maligni spiritus affectent* [it is impossible to describe the ardour with which evil spirits seek to obtain dominion over men and the honours of divine worship]. Trithemius, in his book *de septem secundis*, assigns names to such angels as are governors of particular provinces, by what authority I know not, and gives them several jurisdictions. Asclepiades a Grecian, Rabbi Achiba the Jew, Abraham Avenezra and Rabbi Azariel, Arabians (as I find them cited by Cicogna), farther add, that they are not our governors only, *sed ex eorum concordia et discordia, boni et mali affectus promanant*, but as they agree, so do we and our princes, or disagree; stand or fall. Juno was a bitter enemy to Troy, Apollo a good friend, Jupiter indifferent, *Æqua Venus Teucris, Pallas iniqua fuit* [Venus was for the Trojans, Pallas against]; some are for us still, some against us, *Premente deo, fert deus alter opem* [when one god threatens, another comes to the rescue]. Religion, policy, public and private quarrels, wars are procured by them, and they are delighted perhaps to see men fight, as men are with cocks, bulls and dogs, bears, etc. Plagues, dearths depend on them, our *bene* and *male esse*, and almost all our other peculiar actions (for as Anthony Rusca contends, *lib. 5, cap.* 18, every man hath a good and a bad angel attending on him in particular all his life long, which Iamblichus calls *dæmonem*), preferments, losses, weddings, deaths, rewards and punishments, and as Proclus will, all offices whatsoever, *alii genetricem, alii opificem potestatem habent* [some help in childbirth, others in manual labours], etc., and several names they give them according to their offices, as *Lares, Indigetes, Præstites*, etc. When the Arcades in that battle at Chæronea, which was fought against King Philip for the liberty of Greece, had deceitfully carried themselves, long after, in the very same place, *diis Græciæ ultoribus* [through the avenging gods of Greece] (saith mine author) they were miserably slain by Metellus the Roman: so likewise, in smaller matters, they will have things fall out, as these *boni* and *mali genii* favour or dislike us. *Saturnini non conveniunt Jovialibus*, etc. He that is *Saturninus* shall never likely be preferred. That base fellows are often advanced, undeserving Gnathos, and vicious parasites, whereas discreet, wise, virtuous and worthy men are neglected and unrewarded, they refer to those domineering spirits, or subordinate genii; as they are inclined, or favour men, so they thrive, are ruled and overcome; for, as Libanius supposeth, in our ordinary conflicts and contentions, *Genius genio cedit et obtemperat*, one genius yields and is overcome by another. All particular events almost they refer to these private spirits; and (as Paracelsus adds) they direct, teach, inspire, and instruct men. Never was any man extraordinary famous in any art, action, or great commander, that had not *familiarem dæmonem* [a familiar spirit] to inform him, as Numa, Socrates, and many such (as Cardan illustrates, *cap.* 128, *Arcanis prudentiæ civilis*); *speciali siquidem gratia se a Deo donari asserunt magi, a geniis cælestibus instrui, ab iis doceri* [the Magians assert that they are vouchsafed from God a special grace, that they are trained and instructed by the heavenly spirits]. But these are most erroneous paradoxes, *ineptæ et fabulosæ nugæ*, rejected by our divines and Christian Churches. 'Tis true they have, by God's permission, power over us, and we find by experience that they can hurt not our fields only, cattle, goods, but our bodies and minds. At Hammel in Saxony, *ann.* 1484, 20 *Junii*, the devil, in likeness of a pied piper, carried away 130 children that were never after seen. Many times men are affrighted out of their wits, carried away quite, as Scheretzius illustrates, *lib.* 1, *cap.* 4, and severally molested by his means. Plotinus the Platonist, *lib.* 14 *advers. Gnost.*, laughs them to scorn that hold the devil or spirits can cause any such diseases. Many think he can work upon the body, but not upon the mind. But experience pronounceth otherwise, that he can work both upon body and mind. Tertullian is of this opinion, *cap.* 22, 'that he can cause both sickness and health,' and that secretly. Taurellus adds, 'By clancular poisons he can infect the bodies, and hinder the operations of the bowels, though we perceive it not,' 'closely creeping into them,' saith Lipsius, and so crucify our souls: *et nociva melancholia furiosos efficit* [and makes people mad from noxious melancholy]. For being a spiritual body, he struggles with our spirits, saith Rogers, and suggests (according to Cardan) *verba sine voce, species sine visu* [words without speaking, sights without showing anything], envy, lust, anger, etc., as he sees men inclined.

The manner how he performs it, Biarmannus, in his Oration against Bodine, sufficiently declares. 'He begins first with the phantasy, and moves that so strongly that no reason is able to resist.' Now the phantasy he moves by mediation of humours; although many physicians are of opinion that the devil can alter the mind, and produce this disease of himself. *Quibusdam medicorum visum*, saith Avicenna, *quod melancholia contingat a dæmonio* [some doctors have held that melancholy is from the devil]. Of the same mind is Psellus, and Rhasis the Arab, *lib.* 1, *tract.* 9, *Cont.*, 'that this disease proceeds especially from the devil, and from him alone.' Arculanus, *cap.* 6, *in* 9 *Rhasis*; Ælianus Montaltus in his 9th *cap.*; Daniel Sennertus, *lib.* 1, *part.* 2, *cap.* 11, confirm as much, that the devil can cause this disease; by reason many times that the parties affected prophesy, speak strange language, but *non sine interventu humoris*, not without the humour, as he interprets himself; no more doth Avicenna: *Si contingat a dæmonio, sufficit nobis ut convertat complexionem ad choleram nigram, et sit causa ejus propinqua cholera nigra* [if it is from the devil, the sufficient sign is that it turns the humour to black bile and that its immediate cause is black bile]; the immediate cause is choler adust, which Pomponatius likewise labours to make good: Galgerandus of Mantua, a famous physician, so cured a dæmoniacal woman in his time, that spake all languages, by purging black choler; and thereupon, belike, this humour of melancholy is called *balneum diaboli*, the devil's bath; the devil, spying his opportunity of such humours, drives them many times to despair, fury, rage, etc., mingling himself amongst these humours. This is that which Tertullian avers, *Corporibus infligunt acerbos casus, animæque repentinos, membra distorquent, occulte repentes* [they cause grievous bodily and mental harm; they distort the limbs, coming on stealthily], etc., and which Lemnius goes about to prove, *Immiscent se mali genii pravis humoribus, atque atræ bili* [evil spirits insert themselves in depraved humours and black bile], etc. And Jason Pratensis, 'that the devil, being a slender incomprehensible spirit, can easily insinuate and wind himself into human bodies, and, cunningly couched in our bowels, vitiate our healths, terrify our souls with fearful dreams, and shake our mind with furies.' And in another place, 'These unclean spirits settled in our bodies, and now mixed with our melancholy humours, do triumph as it were, and sport themselves as in another heaven.' Thus he argues, and that they go in and out of our bodies, as bees do in a hive, and so provoke and tempt us as they perceive our temperature inclined of itself, and most apt to be deluded. Agrippa and Lavater are persuaded that this humour invites the devil to it, wheresoever it is in extremity, and, of all other, melancholy persons are most subject to diabolical temptations and illusions, and most apt to entertain them, and the devil best able to work upon them. But whether by obsession, or possession, or otherwise, I will not determine; 'tis a difficult question. Delrio the Jesuit, *tom.* 3, *lib.* 6; Sprenger and his colleague, *Mall. Malef.*; Pet. Thyræus the Jesuit, *lib. de dæmoniacis, de locis infestis, de terrificationibus nocturnis*; Hieronymus Mengus, *Flagel. dæm.*, and others of that rank of pontifical writers, it seems, by their exorcisms and conjurations approve of it, having forged many stories to that purpose. A nun did eat a lettuce without grace or signing it with the sign of the cross, and was instantly possessed. Durand, *lib.* 6 *Rational. cap.* 86, *num.* 8, relates that he saw a wench possessed in Bononia with two devils, by eating an unhallowed pomegranate, as she did afterwards confess, when she was cured by exorcisms. And therefore our papists do sign themselves so often with the sign of the cross, *ne dæmon ingredi ausit* [that the demon may not dare to enter], and exorcise all manner of meats, as being unclean or accursed otherwise, as Bellarmine defends. Many such stories I find amongst pontifical writers, to prove their assertions; let them free their own credits; some few I will recite in this kind out of most approved physicians. Cornelius Gemma, *lib.* 2 *de nat. mirac. cap.* 4, related of a young maid, called Katherine Gualter, a cooper's daughter, *anno* 1571, that had such strange passions and convulsions, three men could not sometimes hold her; she purged a live eel, which he saw, a foot and a half long, and touched himself; but the eel afterwards vanished; she vomited some twenty-four pounds of fulsome stuff of all colours, twice a day for fourteen days; and after that she voided great balls of hair, pieces of wood, pigeon's dung, parchment, goose dung, coals; and after them two pound of pure blood, and then again coals and stones, of which some had inscriptions, bigger than a walnut, some of them pieces of glass, brass, etc., besides paroxysms of laughing, weeping and ecstasies, etc. *Et hoc (inquit) cum horrore vidi,* 'this I saw with horror.' They could do no good on her by physic, but left her to the clergy. Marcellus Donatus, *lib.* 2, *cap.* I, *de med. mirab.*, hath such another story of a country fellow, that had four knives in his belly, *instar serræ dentatos*, indented like a saw, every one a span long, and a wreath of hair like a globe, with much baggage of like sort, wonderful to behold: how it should come into his guts, he concludes, *certo non alio quam dæmonis astutia et dolo* [could assuredly only have been through the artifice of the devil]. Langius, *Epist. med. lib.* I, *epist.* 38, hath many relations to this effect, and so hath Christopherus à Vega: Wierus, Sckenkius, Scribanius, all agree that they are done by the subtlety and illusion of the devil. If you shall ask a reason of this, 'tis to exercise our patience; for as Tertullian holds, *Virtus non est virtus, nisi comparem habet aliquem, in quo superando vim suam ostendat* [virtue is not worthy of the name till it has overcome an antagonist worthy of its steel]; 'tis to try us and our faith, 'tis for our offences, and for the punishment of our sins, by God's permission they do it, *carnifices vindictæ justæ Dei,* as Tholosanus styles them, executioners of His will; or rather as David (Ps. lxxviii, 49), 'He cast upon them the fierceness of his anger, indignation, wrath, and vexation, by sending out of evil angels'; so did He afflict Job, Saul, the lunatics and dæmoniacal persons whom Christ cured (Matt. iv, 8; Luke iv, II; Luke xiii; Mark ix; Tobit viii, 3, etc.). This, I say, happeneth for a punishment of sin, for their want of faith, incredulity, weakness, distrust, etc.

Old Age a Cause

Secondary peculiar causes efficient, so called in respect of the other precedent, are either *congenitæ, internæ, innatæ*, as they term them, inward, innate, inbred; or else outward and adventitious, which happen to us after we are born: congenite, or born with us, are either natural, as old age, or *præter naturam* [unnatural] (as Fernelius calls it), that distemperature which we have from our parents' seed, it being an hereditary disease. The first of these, which is natural to all, and which no man living can avoid, is old age, which being cold and dry, and of the same quality as melancholy is, must needs cause it, by diminution of spirits and substance, and increasing of adust humours; therefore Melancthon avers out of Aristotle, as an undoubted truth, *senes plerumque delirasse in senecta*, that old men familiarly dote, *ob atram bilem*, for black choler, which is then superabundant in them: and Rhasis, that Arabian physician, in his *Cont. lib.* 1, *cap.* 9, calls it 'a necessary and inseparable accident' to all old and decrepit persons. After seventy years (as the Psalmist saith) 'all is trouble and sorrow'; and common experience confirms the truth of it in weak and old persons, especially such as have lived in action all their lives, had great employment, much business, much command, and many servants to oversee, and leave off *ex abrupto*, as Charles the Fifth did to King Philip, resign up all on a sudden; they are overcome with melancholy in an instant: or if they do continue in such courses, they dote at last (*senex bis puer* [an old man is in his second boyhood]), and are not able to manage their estates through common infirmities incident in their age; full of ache, sorrow, and grief, children again, dizzards, they carle many times as they sit, and talk to themselves, they are angry, waspish, displeased with everything, 'suspicious of all, wayward, covetous, hard' (saith Tully), 'self-willed, superstitious, self-conceited, braggers, and admirers of themselves,' as Balthasar Castilio hath truly noted of them. This natural infirmity is most eminent in old women, and such as are poor, solitary, live in most base esteem and beggary, or such as are witches; in-somuch that Wierus, Baptista Porta, Ulricus Molitor, Edwicus, do refer all that witches are said to do, to imagination alone, and this humour of melancholy. And whereas it is controverted, whether they can bewitch cattle to death, ride in the air upon a cowl-staff out of a chimney-top, transform themselves into cats, dogs, etc., translate bodies from place to place, meet in companies and dance, as they do, or have carnal copulation with the devil, they ascribe all to this redundant melancholy, which domineers in them, to somniferous potions, and natural causes, the devil's policy. *Non lædunt omnino* (saith Wierus) *aut quid mirum faciunt (de Lamiis, lib.* 3, *cap.* 36), *ut putatur, solam vitiatam habent phantasiam*; they do no such wonders at all, only their brains are crazed. 'They think they are witches, and can do hurt, but do not.' But this opinion Bodine, Erastus, Danæus, Scribanius, Sebastian Michaelis, Campanella, *de sensu rerum, lib.* 4, *cap.* 9, Dandinus the Jesuit, *lib.* 2 *de Anima*, explode; Cicogna confutes at large. That witches are melancholy they deny not, but not out of a corrupt phantasy alone, so to delude themselves and others, or to produce such effects.

Parents a Cause by Propagation

That other inward, inbred cause of melancholy is our temperature, in whole or part, which we receive from our parents, which Fernelius calls *præter naturam*, or unnatural, it being an hereditary disease; for as he justifies, *Quale parentum maxime patris semen obtigerit, tales evadunt similares spermaticæque partes, quocunque etiam morbo pater quum generat tenetur, cum semine transfert in prolem*; such as the temperature of the father is, such is the son's, and look what disease the father had when he · begot him, his son will have after him; 'and is as well inheritor of his infirmities as of his lands.' 'And where the complexion and constitution of the father is corrupt, there' (saith Roger Bacon) 'the complexion and constitution of the son must needs be corrupt, and so the corruption is derived from the father to the son.' Now this doth not so much appear in the composition of the body, according to that of Hippocrates, 'in habit, proportion, scars, and other lineaments; but in manners and conditions of the mind,' *Et patrum in natos abeunt cum semine mores* [the character of the parents is transmitted to the children through the seed].

Selecus had an anchor on his thigh, so had his posterity, as Trogus records, *lib.* 15. Lepidus, in Pliny, *lib.* 7, *cap.* 17, was purblind, so was his son. That famous family of Aenobarbi were known of old, and so surnamed from their red beards; the Austrian lip, and those Indians' flat noses are propagated, the Bavarian chin, and goggle eyes amongst the Jews, as Buxtorfius observes; their voice, pace, gesture, looks, is likewise derived with all the rest of their conditions and infirmities; such a mother, such a daughter; their very affections Lemnius contends 'to follow their seed, and the malice and bad conditions of children are many times wholly to be imputed to their parents'; I need not therefore make any doubt of melancholy, but that it is an hereditary disease. Paracelsus in express words affirms it, *lib. de morb. amentium, to. 4, tr.* 1; so doth Crato in an epistle of his to Monavius. So doth Bruno Seidelius in his book *de morbo incurab.* Montaltus proves, *cap.* II, out of Hippocrates and Plutarch, that such hereditary dispositions are frequent, *et hanc (inquit) fieri reor ob participation melancholicam intemperantiam* (speaking of a patient), 'I think he became so by participation of melancholy.' Daniel Sennertus, *lib.* 1, *part.* 2, *cap.* 9, will have his melancholy constitution derived not only from the father to the son, but to the whole family sometimes: *quandoque totis familiis hæreditativam.* Forestus, in his medicinal observations, illustrates this point, with an example of a merchant, his patient, that had this infirmity by inheritance; so doth Rodericus à Fonseca, *tom.* 1, *consul.* 69, by an instance of a young man that was so affected *ex matre melancholica*, had a melancholy mother, *et victu melancholico*, and bad diet together. Lodovicus Mercatus, a Spanish physician, in that excellent tract which he hath lately written of hereditary diseases, *tom.* 2 *oper. lib.* 5, reckons up leprosy, as those Galbots in Gascony, hereditary lepers, pox, stone,

gout, epilepsy, etc. Amongst the rest, this and madness
after a set time comes to many, which he calls a miraculous thing in nature, and sticks for ever to them as an
incurable habit. And that which is more to be wondered
at, it skips in some families the father, and goes to the
son, 'or takes every other, and sometimes every third in
a lineal descent, and doth not always produce the same,
but some like, and a symbolizing disease.' These secondary causes hence derived are commonly so powerful,
that (as Wolfius holds) *sæpe mutant decreta siderum,*
they do often alter the primary causes, and decrees of
the heavens. For these reasons, belike, the Church and
commonwealth, human and divine laws, have conspired
to avoid hereditary diseases, forbidding such marriages
as are any whit allied; and as Mercatus adviseth all
families to take such, *si fieri possit, quæ maxime distant
natura* [if possible, as are most distant in nature], and to
make choice of those that are most differing in complexion from them, if they love their own, and respect
the common good. And sure, I think, it hath been ordered
by God's especial providence, that in all ages there should
be (as usually there is) once in six hundred years, a
transmigration of nations, to amend and purify their
blood, as we alter seed upon our land, and that there
should be, as it were, an inundation of those northern
Goths and Vandals, and many such-like people which
came out of that continent of Scandia and Sarmatia (as
some suppose) and overran, as a deluge, most part of
Europe and Africa, to alter for our good our complexions,
which were much defaced with hereditary infirmities,
which by our lust and intemperance we had contracted.

A sound generation of strong and able men were sent amongst us, as those northern men usually are, innocuous, free from riot, and free from diseases; to qualify and make us as those poor naked Indians are generally at this day, and those about Brazil (as a late writer observes), in the Isle of Maragnan, free from all hereditary diseases or other contagion, whereas without help of physic they live commonly 120 years or more, as in the Orcades and many other places. Such are the common effects of temperance and intemperance; but I will descend to particulars, and show by what means, and by whom especially, this infirmity is derived unto us.

Filii ex senibus nati, raro sunt firmi temperamenti, old men's children are seldom of a good temperament, as Scoltzius supposeth, *consult*. 177, and therefore most apt to this disease; and as Levinus Lemnius farther adds, old men beget most part wayward, peevish, sad, melancholy sons, and seldom merry. He that begets a child on a full stomach will either have a sick child or a crazed son (as Cardan thinks, *Contradict. med. lib.* 1, *contradict.* 18), or if the parents be sick, or have any great pain of the head, or megrim, headache (Hieronymus Wolfius doth instance in a child of Sebastian Castalio's), or if a drunken man get a child, it will never likely have a good brain, as Gellius argues, *lib.* 12, *cap.* 1. *Ebrii gignunt ebrios*, one drunkard begets another, saith Plutarch, *Symp. lib.* 1, *quest.* 5, whose sentence Lemnius approves, *lib.* 1, *cap.* 4; Alsarius Crucius Gen., *de quæsit. med. cent.* 3, *fol.* 182; Macrobius, *lib.* 1; Avicenna, *lib.* 3, *fen.* 21, *tract.* 1, *cap.* 8; and Aristotle himself, *sect.* 2, *prob.* 4. Foolish, drunken, or hairbrain women most part bring forth children like unto themselves, *morosos et languidos* [morose and feeble], and so likewise he that lies with a menstruous woman. *Intemperantia veneris, quam in nautis præsertim insectatur Lemnius, qui uxores ineunt, nulla menstrui decursus ratione habita, nec observato interlunio, præcipua causa est, noxia, perniciosa (concubitum hunc exitialem ideo, et pestiferum vocat Rodericus a Castro, Lusitanus, detestantur ad unum omnes medici), tum et quarta luna concepti, infelices plerumque et amentes, deliri, stolidi, morbosi, impuri, invalidi, tetra lue sordidi, minime vitales, omnibus bonis corporis atque animi destituti: ad laborem nati, si seniores, inquit Eustathius, ut Hercules, et alii. Judæi maxime insectantur fædum hunc et immundum apud Christianos concubitum, ut illicitum abhorrent, et apud suos prohibent; et quod Christiani toties leprosi, amentes, tot morbilli, impetigines, alphi, psoræ, cutis et faciei decolorationes, tam multi morbi epidemici, acerbi, et venenosi sint, in hunc immundum concubitum rejiciunt, et crudeles in pignora vocant, qui quarta luna profluente hac mensium illuvie concubitum hunc non perhorrescunt. Damnavit olim divina lex et morte mulctavit hujusmodi homines* (Lev. xviii, xx), *et inde nati, si qui deformes aut mutili, pater dilapidatus, quod non contineret ab immunda muliere. Gregorius Magnus, petenti Augustino numquid apud Britannos hujusmodi concubitum toleraret, severe prohibuit viris suis tum misceri feminas in consuetis suis menstruis, etc.* I spare to English this which I have said. Another cause some give, inordinate diet, as if a man eat garlic, onions, fast overmuch, study too hard, be over-sorrowful, dull, heavy, dejected in mind, perplexed in his thoughts, fearful, etc., 'their children' (saith Cardan, *Subtil. lib.* 18) 'will be much subject to madness and melancholy; for if the spirits of the brain be fuzzled or misaffected by such means at such a time, their children will be fuzzled in the brain: they will be dull, heavy, timorous, discontented all their lives.' Some are of opinion, and maintain that paradox or problem, that wise men beget commonly fools; Suidas gives instance in Aristarchus the Grammarian, *duos reliquit filios, Aristarchum et Aristachorum, ambos stultos* [he left two sons, Aristarchus and Aristachorus, both stupid]; and which Erasmus urgeth in his *Moria*, fools beget wise men. Cardan, *Subt. lib.* 12, gives this cause, *quoniam spiritus sapientum ob studium resolvuntur, et in cerebrum feruntur a corde*: because their natural spirits are resolved by study, and turned into animal; drawn from the heart, and those other parts, to the brain. Lemnius subscribes to that of Cardan, and assigns this reason, *quod persolvant debitum languide, et oscitanter, unde fœtus a parentum genero-sitate desciscit*: they pay their debt (as Paul calls it) to their wives remissly, by which means their children are weaklings, and many times idiots and fools.

Some other causes are given, which properly pertain to, and do proceed from, the mother. If she be over-dull, heavy, angry, peevish, discontented, and melancholy, not only at the time of conception, but even all the while she carries the child in her womb (saith Fernelius, *Path. lib.* 1, 11), her son will be so likewise affected, and worse, as Lemnius adds, *lib.* 4, *cap.* 7. If she grieve overmuch, be disquieted, or by any casualty be affrighted and terri-fied by some fearful object heard or seen, she endangers her child, and spoils the temperature of it; for the strange imagination of a woman works effectually upon her infant, that, as Baptista Porta proves, *Physiog. cœlestis, lib.* 5, *cap.* 2, she leaves a mark upon it, which is most especially seen in such as prodigiously long for such and such meats; the child will love those meats, saith Fernelius, and be addicted to like humours: 'if a great-bellied woman see a hare, her child will often have an hare-lip,' as we call it. Garcæus, *de judiciis geniturarum, cap.* 33, hath a memorable example of one Thomas Nickell, born in the city of Brandenburg, 1551, 'that went reeling and staggering all the days of his life, as if he would fall to the ground, because his mother being great with child saw a drunken man reeling in the street.' Such another I find in Martin Wenrichius, *Com. de ortu monstrorum, cap.* 17. 'I saw' (saith he) 'at Wittenberg, in Germany, a citizen that looked like a carcass; I asked him the cause, he replied, 'His mother, when she bore him in her womb, saw a carcass by chance, and was so sore affrighted with it, that *ex eo fœtus ei assimilatus*, from a ghastly impression the child was like it.'

So many several ways are we plagued and punished for our fathers' defaults; insomuch that, as Fernelius truly saith, 'It is the greatest part of our felicity to be well born, and it were happy for humankind, if only such parents as are sound of body and mind should be suffered to marry.' An husbandman will sow none but the best and choicest seed upon his land, he will not rear a bull or a horse, except he be right shapen in all parts, or permit him to cover a mare, except he be well assured of his breed; we make choice of the best rams for our sheep, rear the neatest kine, and keep the best dogs, *quanto id diligentius in procreandis liberis observandum!* and how careful then should we be in begetting of our

children! In former times some countries have been so
chary in this behalf, so stern, that if a child were crooked
or deformed in body or mind, they made him away: so
did the Indians of old by the relation of Curtius, and
many other well-governed commonwealths, according
to the discipline of those times. Heretofore in Scotland,
saith Hect. Boethius, 'if any were visited with the falling
sickness, madness, gout, leprosy, or any such dangerous
disease, which was likely to be propagated from the
father to the son, he was instantly gelded; a woman kept
from all company of men; and if by chance, having some
such disease, she were found to be with child, she with
her brood were buried alive: and this was done for the
common good, lest the whole nation should be injured
or corrupted.' A severe doom, you will say, and not to
be used amongst Christians, yet more to be looked into
than it is. For now, by our too much facility in this kind,
in giving way for all to marry that will, too much liberty
and indulgence in tolerating all sorts, there is a vast
confusion of hereditary diseases, no family secure, no
man, almost, free from some grievous infirmity or other,
when no choice is had, but still the eldest must marry,
as so many stallions of the race; or if rich, be they
fools or dizzards, lame or maimed, unable, intemperate,
dissolute, exhaust through riot, as he said, *jure hæreditario
sapere jubentur*; they must be wise and able by inheritance:
it comes to pass that our generation is corrupt, we have
many weak persons, both in body and mind, many
feral diseases raging amongst us, crazed families, *parentes
peremptores* [our parents are our ruin], our fathers bad,
and we are like to be worse.

Bad Diet a Cause – Substance.
Quality of Meats

According to my proposed method, having opened hitherto these secondary causes, which are inbred with us, I must now proceed to the outward and adventitious, which happen unto us after we are born. And those are either evident, remote, or inward, antecedent, and the nearest: continent causes some call them. These outward, remote, precedent causes are subdivided again into necessary and not necessary. Necessary (because we cannot avoid them, but they will alter us, as they are used or abused) are those six non-natural things, so much spoken of amongst physicians, which are principal causes of this disease. For almost in every consultation, whereas they shall come to speak of the causes, the fault is found, and this most part objected to the patient: *Peccavit circa res sex non naturales*, he hath still offended in one of those six. Montanus, *consil.* 22, consulted about a melancholy Jew, gives that sentence, so did Frisimelica in the same place; and in his 244th counsel, censuring a melancholy soldier, assigns that reason of his malady, 'He offended in all those six non-natural things, which were the outward causes, from which came those inward obstructions'; and so in the rest.

These six non-natural things are diet, retention, and evacuation, which are more material than the other because they make new matter, or else are conversant in keeping or expelling of it; the other four are air, exercise, sleeping, waking, and perturbations of the mind, which only alter the matter. The first of these is diet, which consists in meat and drink, and causeth melancholy, as it offends in substance or accidents, that is quantity, quality, or the like. And well it may be called a material cause, since that, as Fernelius holds, 'it hath such a power in begetting of diseases, and yields the matter and sustenance of them; for neither air, nor perturbations, nor any of those other evident causes take place, or work this effect, except the constitution of body and preparation of humours do concur; that a man may say this diet is the mother of diseases, let the father be what he will; and from this alone melancholy and frequent other maladies arise.' Many physicians, I confess, have written copious volumes of this one subject, of the nature and qualities of all manner of meats; as namely, Galen, Isaac the Jew; Halyabbas, Avicenna, Mesue, also four Arabians; Gordonius, Villanovanus, Wecker, Johannes Bruerinus, *Sitologia de Esculentis et Poculentis*, Michael Savonarola, *tract.* 2, *cap.* 8, Anthony Fumanellus, *lib. de regimine senum*, Curio in his Comment on Schola Salerna, Godefridus Stegius *Arte med.*, Marsilius Cognatus, Ficinus, Ranzovius, Fonseca, Lessius, Magninus, *Regim. sanitatis*, Freitagius, Hugo Fridevallius, etc., besides many other in English; and almost every peculiar physician discourseth at large of all peculiar meats in his chapter of melancholy: yet because these books are not at hand to every man, I will briefly touch of what kind of meats engender this humour, through their several species, and which are to be avoided. How they alter and change the matter, spirits first, and after humours, by which we are preserved, and the constitution of our body, Fernelius and others will show you. I hasten to the thing itself: and first of such diet as offends in substance.

Beef, a strong and hearty meat (cold in the first degree, dry in the second, saith Galen, *lib.* 3, *cap.* 1, *de alim. fac.*), is condemned by him and all succeeding authors to breed gross melancholy blood: good for such as are sound and of a strong constitution, for labouring men if ordered aright, corned, young, of an ox (for all gelded meats in every species are held best), or if old, such as have been tired out with labour are preferred. Aubanus and Sabellicus commend Portugal beef to be the most savoury, best and easiest of digestion; we commend ours: but all is rejected and unfit for such as lead a resty life, anyways inclined to melancholy, or dry of complexion; *Tales* (Galen thinks) *de facili melancholicis ægritudinibus capiuntur* [such easily fall a prey to the ailments of melancholy].

Pork, of all meats, is most nutritive in his own nature, but altogether unfit for such as live at ease, are anyways unsound of body or mind: too moist, full of humours, and therefore *noxia delicatis*, saith Savonarola, *ex earum usu ut dubitetur an febris quartana generetur*: naught for queasy stomachs, insomuch that frequent use of it may breed a quartan ague.

Savonarola discommends goat's flesh, and so doth Bruerinus, *lib.* 13, *cap.* 19, calling it a filthy beast, and rammish: and therefore supposeth it will breed rank and filthy substance; yet kid, such as are young and tender,

Isaac accepts, Bruerinus, and Galen, *lib.* 1, *cap.* 1, *de alimentorum facultatibus*.

Hart and red deer hath an evil name: it yields gross nutriment: a strong and great-grained meat, next unto a horse. Which, although some countries eat, as Tartars, and they of China, yet Galen condemns. Young foals are as commonly eaten in Spain as red deer, and to furnish their navies, about Malaga especially, often used; but such meats ask long baking or seething to qualify them, and yet all will not serve.

All venison is melancholy, and begets bad blood; a pleasant meat: in great esteem with us (for we have more parks in England than there are in all Europe besides) in our solemn feasts. 'Tis somewhat better hunted than otherwise, and well prepared by cookery; but generally bad, and seldom to be used.

Hare, a black meat, melancholy, and hard of digestion; it breeds *incubus*, often eaten, and causeth fearful dreams, so doth all venison, and is condemned by a jury of physicians. Mizaldus and some others say that hare is a merry meat, and that it will make one fair, as Martial's epigram testifies to Gellia; but this is *per accidens*, because of the good sport it makes, merry company and good discourse that is commonly at the eating of it, and not otherwise to be understood.

Conies are of the nature of hares. Magninus compares them to beef, pig, and goat, *Reg. sanit. part.* 3, *cap.* 17; yet young rabbits by all men are approved to be good.

Generally, all such meats as are hard of digestion breed melancholy. Aretæus, *lib.* 7, *cap.* 5, reckons up heads and feet, bowels, brains, entrails, marrow, fat, blood, skins, and those inward parts, as heart, lungs, liver, spleen, etc. They are rejected by Isaac, *lib.* 2, *part.* 3; Magninus, *part.* 3, *cap.* 17; Bruerinus, *lib.* 12; Savonarola, *rub.* 32, *tract.* 2.

Milk, and all that comes of milk, as butter and cheese, curds, etc., increase melancholy (whey only excepted, which is most wholesome): some except asses' milk. The rest, to such as are sound, is nutritive and good, especially for young children, but because soon turned to corruption, not good for those that have unclean stomachs, are subject to headache, or have green wounds, stone, etc. Of all cheeses, I take that kind which we call Banbury cheese to be the best; *ex vetustis pessimus*, the older, stronger, and harder, the worst, as Langius discourseth in his epistle to Melancthon, cited by Mizaldus, Isaac, *part.* 5, Galen, *lib.* 3, *de cibis boni succi*, etc.

Amongst fowl, peacocks and pigeons, all fenny fowl are forbidden, as ducks, geese, swans, herons, cranes, coots, didappers, waterhens, with all those teals, currs, sheldrakes, and peckled fowls, that come hither in winter out of Scandia, Muscovy, Greenland, Friesland, which half the year are covered all over with snow and frozen up. Though these be fair in feathers, pleasant in taste, and have a good outside, like hypocrites, white in plumes, and soft, their flesh is hard, black, unwholesome, dangerous, melancholy meat; *Gravant et putrefaciunt stomachum* [they overload and spoil the stomach], saith Isaac, *part.* 5, *de vol.*; their young ones are more tolerable, but young pigeons he quite disapproves.

Rhasis and Magninus discommend all fish, and say they breed viscosities, slimy nutriment, little and humorous nourishment. Savonarola adds cold; moist and phlegmatic, Isaac; and therefore unwholesome for all cold and melancholy complexions: others make a difference, rejecting only, amongst freshwater fish, eel, tench, lamprey, crawfish (which Bright approves, *cap.* 6), and such as are bred in muddy and standing waters, and have a taste of mud, as Franciscus Bonsuetus poetically defines, *lib. de aquatilibus*:

> *Nam pisces omnes, qui stagna lacusque frequentant,*
> *Semper plus succi deterioris habent.*

> All fish, that standing pools and lakes frequent,
> Do ever yield bad juice and nourishment.

Lampreys, Paulus Jovius, *cap.* 34, *de piscibus fluvial.*, highly magnifies, and saith, none speak against them, but *inepti* [fools] and *scrupulosi*, some scrupulous persons; but eels, *cap.* 33, 'he abhorreth in all places, at all times, all physicians detest them, especially about the solstice.' Gomesius, *lib.* 1, *cap.* 22, *de sale*, doth immoderately extol sea-fish, which others as much vilify, and above the rest, dried, soused, indurate fish, as ling, fumadoes, red-herrings, sprats, stock-fish, haberdine, poor-john, all shell-fish. Tim. Bright excepts lobster and crab. Messarius commends salmon, which Bruerinus contradicts, *lib.* 22, *cap.* 17. Magninus rejects conger, sturgeon, turbot, mackerel, skate.

Carp is a fish of which I know not what to determine. Franciscus Bonsuetus accounts it a muddy fish. Hippolytus Salvianus, in his book *de piscium natura et præparatione*, which was printed at Rome in folio, 1554, with most elegant pictures, esteems carp no better than a slimy, watery meat. Paulus Jovius, on the other side, disallowing tench, approves of it; so doth Dubravius in his books of Fish-ponds. Freitagius extols it for an excellent, wholesome meat, and puts it amongst the fishes of the best rank; and so do most of our country gentlemen, that store their ponds almost with no other fish. But this controversy is easily decided, in my judgment, by Bruerinus, *lib.* 22, *cap.* 13. The difference riseth from the site and nature of pools, sometimes muddy, sometimes sweet; they are in taste as the place is from whence they be taken. In like manner almost we may conclude of other fresh fish. But see more in Rondeletius, Bellonius, Oribasius, *lib.* 7, *cap.* 22, Isaac, *lib.* 1, especially Hippolytus Salvianus, who is *instar omnium solus*, etc. Howsoever they may be wholesome and approved, much use of them is not good; P. Forestus, in his Medicinal Observations, relates that Carthusian friars, whose living is most part fish, are more subject to melancholy than any other Order, and that he found by experience, being sometime their physician ordinary at Delft, in Holland. He exemplifies it with an instance of one Buscodnese, a Carthusian of a ruddy colour, and well liking, that by solitary living and fish-eating became so misaffected.

Amongst herbs to be eaten I find gourds, cucumbers, coleworts, melons, disallowed, but especially cabbage. It causeth troublesome dreams, and sends up black vapours to the brain. Galen, *Loc. affect. lib.* 3, *cap.* 6, of all herbs condemns cabbage; and Isaac, *lib.* 2, *cap.* 1, *animæ gravitatem facit*, it brings heaviness to the soul. Some are of opinion that all raw herbs and sallets breed melancholy blood, except bugloss and lettuce. Crato, *consil.* 21, *lib.* 2, speaks against all herbs and worts, except borage, bugloss, fennel, parsley, dill, balm, succory; Magninus, *Regim. sanitatis, part.* 3, *cap.* 31, *Omnes herbæ simpliciter malæ, via cibi*; all herbs are simply evil to feed on (as he thinks). So did that scoffing cook in Plautus hold:

> *Non ego cœnam condio ut alii coqui solent,*
> *Qui mihi condita prata in patinis proferunt,*
> *Boves qui convivas faciunt, herbasque aggerunt.*

> Like other cooks I do not supper dress,
>   That put whole meadows into a platter,
> And make no better of their guests than beeves,
>   With herbs and grass to feed them fatter.

Our Italians and Spaniards do make a whole dinner of herbs and sallets (which our said Plautus calls *cœnas terrestres* [earthy meals], Horace, *cœnas sine sanguine* [bloodless meals]), by which means, as he follows it:

> *Hic homines tam brevem vitam colunt . . .*
> *Qui herbas hujusmodi in alvum suum congerunt,*
> *Formidolosum dictu, non esu modo,*
> *Quas herbas pecudes non edunt, homines edunt.*

> Their lives, that eat such herbs, must needs be short,
> And 'tis a fearful thing for to report,
> That men should feed on such a kind of meat,
> Which very juments would refuse to eat.

They are windy, and not fit, therefore, to be eaten of all men raw, though qualified with oil, but in broths, or otherwise. See more of these in every husbandman and herbalist.

Roots, *etsi quorundam gentium opes sint*, saith Bruerinus, the wealth of some countries, and sole food, are windy and bad, or troublesome to the head: as onions, garlic, scallions, turnips, carrots, radishes, parsnips: Crato, *lib. 2, consil.* 11, disallows all roots, though some approve of parsnips and potatoes. Magninus is of Crato's opinion, 'They trouble the mind, sending gross fumes to the brain, make men mad,' especially garlic, onions, if a man liberally feed on them a year together. Guianerius, *tract.* 15, *cap.* 2, complains of all manner of roots, and so doth Bruerinus, even parsnips themselves, which are the best, *lib. 9, cap.* 14, *Pastinacarum usus succos gignit improbos* [indulgence in parsnips creates harmful juices]. Crato, *consil.* 21, *lib.* 1, utterly forbids all manner of fruits, as pears, apples, plums, cherries, strawberries, nuts, medlars, serves, etc. *Sanguinem inficiunt*, saith Villanovanus, they infect the blood, and putrefy it, Magninus holds, and must not therefore be taken *via cibi, aut quantitate magna*, not to make a meal of, or in any great quantity. Cardan makes that a cause of their continual sickness at Fez in Africa, 'because they live so much on fruits, eating them thrice a day.' Laurentius approves of many fruits, in his Tract of Melancholy, which others disallow, and amongst the rest apples, which some likewise commend, sweetings, pearmains, pippins, as good against melancholy; but to him that is any way inclined to, or touched with this malady, Nicholas Piso, in his Practics, forbids all fruits, as windy, or to be sparingly eaten at least, and not raw. Amongst other fruits, Bruerinus, out of Galen, excepts grapes and figs, but I find them likewise rejected.

All pulse are naught, beans, pease, fitches, etc., they fill the brain (saith Isaac) with gross fumes, breed black, thick blood, and cause troublesome dreams. And therefore, that which Pythagoras said to his scholars of old may be for ever applied to melancholy men, *A fabis abstinete*, eat no pease, nor beans; yet to such as will needs eat them, I would give this counsel, to prepare them according to those rules that Arnoldus Villanovanus and Freitagius prescribe, for eating, and dressing, fruits, herbs, roots, pulse, etc.

Spices cause hot and head melancholy, and are for that cause forbidden by our physicians to such men as are inclined to this malady, as pepper, ginger, cinnamon, cloves, mace, dates, etc., honey, and sugar. Some except honey; to those that are cold it may be tolerable, but *Dulcia se in bilem vertunt* [sweets turn into bile], they are obstructive. Crato therefore forbids all spice, in a consultation of his, for a melancholy schoolmaster, *omnia aromatica, et quicquid sanguinem adurit* [all spices, and whatever dries up the blood]: so doth Fernelius, *consil.* 45; Guianerius, *tract.* 15, *cap.* 2; Mercurialis, *cons.* 189. To these I may add all sharp and sour things, luscious and over-sweet, or fat, as oil, vinegar, verjuice, mustard, salt; as sweet things are obstructive, so these are corrosive. Gomesius, in his books *de sale, lib.* 1, *cap.* 21, highly commends salt; so doth Codronchus in his tract *de sale absinthii*, Lemn. *lib.* 3, *cap.* 9, *de occult. nat. mir.*; yet common experience finds salt, and salt-meats, to be great procurers of this disease. And for that cause belike those Egyptian priests abstained from salt, even so much as in their bread, *ut sine perturbatione anima esset*, saith mine author, that their souls might be free from perturbations.

Bread that is made of baser grain, as pease, beans, oats, rye, or over-hard baked, crusty, and black, is often spoken against, as causing melancholy juice and wind. Joh. Major, in the first book of his History of Scotland, contends much for the wholesomeness of oaten bread: it was objected to him, then living at Paris in France, that his countrymen fed on oats and base grain, as a disgrace; but he doth ingenuously confess, Scotland, Wales, and a third part of England did most part use that kind of bread, that it was as wholesome as any grain, and yielded as good nourishment. And yet Wecker, out of Galen, calls it horse-meat, and fitter for juments than men to feed on. But read Galen himself, *lib.* 1 *de cibis boni et mali succi*, more largely discoursing of corn and bread.

All black wines, over-hot, compound, strong, thick drinks, as muscadine, malmsey, alicant, rumney, brown bastard, metheglin, and the like, of which they have thirty several kinds in Muscovy, all such made drinks are hurtful in this case, to such as are hot, or of a sanguine, choleric complexion, young, or inclined to head-melancholy. For many times the drinking of wine alone causeth it. Arculanus, *cap.* 16, *in* 9 *Rhasis*, puts in wine for a great cause, especially if it be immoderately used. Guianerius, *tract.* 15, *cap.* 2, tells a story of two Dutchmen, to whom he gave entertainment in his house, 'that in one month's space were both melancholy by drinking of wine, one did naught but sing, the other sigh.' Galen, *lib. de causis morb., cap.* 3; Matthiolus on Dioscorides; and above all other Andreas Bachius, *lib.* 3, *cap.* 18, 19, 20, have reckoned upon those inconveniences that come by wine: yet notwithstanding all this, to such as are cold, or sluggish melancholy, a cup of wine is good physic, and so doth Mercurialis grant, *consil.* 25; in that case, if the temperature be cold, as to most melancholy men it is, wine is much commended, if it be moderately used.

Cider and perry are both cold and windy drinks, and for that cause to be neglected, and so are all those hot, spiced, strong drinks.

Beer, if it be over-new, or over-stale, over-strong, or not sod, smell of the cask, sharp, or sour, is most unwholesome, frets, and galls, etc. Henricus Ayrerus, in a consultation of his, for one that laboured of hypochondriacal melancholy, discommends beer. So doth Crato, in that excellent counsel of his, *lib.* 2, *consil.* 21, as too windy, because of the hop. But he means, belike, that thick, black Bohemian beer used in some other parts of Germany:

Nil spissius illa
Dum bibitur, nil clarius est dum mingitur, unde
Constat, quod multas fæces in corpore linquat.

Nothing comes in so thick,
Nothing goes out so thin,
It must needs follow then
The dregs are left within.

As that old poet scoffed, calling it *Stygiæ monstrum conforme paludi,* a monstrous drink, like the River Styx. But let them say as they list, to such as are accustomed unto it, ''tis a most wholesome' (so Polydore Virgil calleth it) 'and a pleasant drink,' it is more subtile and better for the hop that rarefies it, hath an especial virtue against melancholy, as our herbalists confess, Fuchsius approves, *lib.* 2, *sec.* 3, *Instit. cap.* 11, and many others.

Standing waters, thick and ill-coloured, such as come forth of pools and moats where hemp hath been steeped or slimy fishes live, are most unwholesome, putrefied, and full of mites, creepers, slimy, muddy, unclean, corrupt, impure, by reason of the sun's heat and still standing; they cause foul distemperatures in the body and mind of man, are unfit to make drink of, to dress meat with, or to be used about men inwardly or outwardly. They are good for many domestic uses, to wash horses, water cattle, etc., or in time of necessity, but not otherwise. Some are of opinion that such fat, standing waters make the best beer, and that seething doth defecate it, as Cardan holds, *lib.* 13 *Subtil.*, 'It mends the substance and savour of it,' but it is a paradox. Such beer may be stronger, but not so wholesome as the other, as Jobertus truly justifieth out of Galen, *Paradox. dec.* 1, *paradox.* 5, that the seething of such impure waters doth not purge or purify them; Pliny, *lib.* 31, *cap.* 3, is of the same tenent, and P. Crescentius, *Agricult. lib.* 1 *et lib.* 4, *cap.* 11 *et cap.* 45. Pamphilius Herilachus, *lib.* 4 *de nat. aquarum*, such waters are naught, not to be used, and by the testimony of Galen, 'breed agues, dropsies, pleurisies, splenetic and melancholy passions, hurt the eyes, cause a bad temperature and ill disposition of the whole body, with bad colour.' This Jobertus stiffly maintains, *Paradox. lib.* 1, *part.* 5, that it causeth blear eyes, bad colour, and many loathsome diseases to such as use it: this which they say, stands with good reason; for as geographers relate, the water of Astracan breeds worms in such as drink it. Axius, or as now called Verduri, the fairest river in Macedonia, makes all cattle black that taste of it. Aliacmon, now Peleca, another stream in Thessaly, turns cattle most part white, *si potui ducas* [if you take them to drink there]. J. Aubanus Bohemus refers that *struma* or poke of the Bavarians and Styrians to the nature of their waters, as Munster doth that of the Valesians in the Alps, and Bodine supposeth the stuttering of some families in Aquitania, about Labden, to proceed from the same cause, 'and that the filth is derived from the water to their bodies.' So that they that use filthy, standing, ill-coloured, thick, muddy water, must needs have muddy, ill-coloured, impure, and infirm bodies. And because the body works upon the mind, they shall have grosser understandings, dull, foggy, melancholy spirits, and be readily subject to all manner of infirmities.

To these noxious simples we may reduce an infinite number of compound, artificial, made dishes, of which our cooks afford us a great variety, as tailors do fashions in our apparel. Such are puddings stuffed with blood, or otherwise composed; baked meats, soused indurate meats, fried and broiled, buttered meats, condite, powdered, and over-dried; all cakes, simnels, buns, cracknels made with butter, spice, etc., fritters, pancakes, pies; sausages, and those several sauces, sharp, or over-sweet, of which *scientia popinæ* [the learning of the cookshop], as Seneca calls it, hath served those Apician tricks and perfumed dishes, which Adrian the Sixth, Pope, so much admired in the accounts of his predecessor Leo Decimus, and which prodigious riot and prodigality have invented in this age. These do generally engender gross humours, fill the stomach with crudities, and all those inward parts with obstructions. Montanus, *consil.* 22, gives instance in a melancholy Jew, that by eating such tart sauces, made dishes, and salt meats, with which he was overmuch delighted, became melancholy, and was evil-affected. Such examples are familiar and common.

Quantity of Diet a Cause

There is not so much harm proceeding from the substance itself of meat, and quality of it, in ill dressing and preparing, as there is from the quantity, disorder of time and place, unseasonable use of it, intemperance, overmuch or overlittle taking of it. A true saying it is, *Plures crapula quam gladius*, this gluttony kills more than the sword, this *omnivorans et homicida gula*, this all-devouring and murdering gut. And that of Pliny is truer, 'Simple diet is the best; heaping up of several meats is pernicious, and sauces worse; many dishes bring many diseases.' Avicen cries out, that 'nothing is worse than to feed on many dishes, or to protract the time of meats longer than ordinary; from thence proceed our infirmities, and 'tis the fountain of all diseases, which arise out of the repugnancy of gross humours.' Thence, saith Fernelius, come crudities, wind, oppilations, cacochymia, plethora, cachexia, bradypepsia, *Hinc subitæ mortes, atque intestata senectus*, sudden death, etc., and what not.

As a lamp is choked with a multitude of oil, or a little fire with overmuch wood quite extinguished, so is the natural heat with immoderate eating strangled in the body. *Perniciosa sentina est abdomen insaturabile*, one saith, an insatiable paunch is a pernicious sink, and the fountain of all diseases, both of body and mind. Mercurialis will have it a peculiar cause of this private disease; Solenander, *consil. 5, sect. 3*, illustrates this of Mercurialis with an example of one so melancholy, *ab intempestivis commessationibus*, [from] unseasonable feasting. Crato confirms as much, in that often cited counsel, 21, *lib. 2*, putting superfluous eating for a main cause. But what need I seek farther for proofs? Hear Hippocrates himself, *lib. 2, aphor. 10*: 'Impure bodies, the more they are nourished, the more they are hurt, for the nourishment is putrefied with vicious humours.'

And yet for all this harm, which apparently follows surfeiting and drunkenness, see how we luxuriate and rage in this kind; read what Johannes Stuckius hath written lately of this subject, in his great volume *de Antiquorum Conviviis*, and of our present age; *Quam portentosæ cœnæ*, [what] prodigious suppers, *Qui dum invitant ad cœnam efferunt ad sepulchrum* [who in inviting us to supper conduct us to our graves], what Fagos, Epicures, Apiciuses, Heliogables, our times afford! Lucullus' ghost walks still, and every man desires to sup in Apollo; Æsop's costly dish is ordinarily served up. *Magis illa juvant, quæ pluris emunter* [the more they cost, the more we enjoy them]. The dearest cates are best, and 'tis an ordinary thing to bestow twenty or thirty pound on a dish, some thousand crowns upon a dinner: Muley-Hamet, King of Fez and Morocco, spent three pounds on the sauce of a capon: it is nothing in our times, we scorn all that is cheap. 'We loathe the very light' (some of us, as Seneca notes) 'because it comes free, and we are offended with the sun's heat, and those cool blasts, because we buy them not.' This air we breathe is so common, we care not for it; nothing pleaseth but what is dear. And if we be witty in anything, it is *ad gulam*; if we study at all, it is *erudito luxu* [the learning of luxury], to please the palate, and to satisfy the gut. 'A cook of old was a base knave' (as Livy complains), 'but now a great man in request; cookery is become an art, a noble science; cooks are gentlemen'; *Venter Deus* [their belly is their god]. They wear 'their brains in their bellies, and their guts in their heads,' as Agrippa taxed some parasites of his time, rushing on their own destruction, as if a man should run upon the point of a sword, *usque dum rumpantur comedunt* [they eat till they burst]: all day, all night, let the physician say what he will, imminent danger and feral diseases are now ready to seize upon them, that will eat till they vomit, *Edunt ut vomant, vomunt ut edant* [they eat to vomit and vomit to eat], saith Seneca (which Dion relates of Vitellius, *Solo transitu ciborum nutriri judicatus:* his meat did pass through and away), or till they burst again. *Strage animantium ventrem onerant* [they load their bellies with the spoil of the animal world], and rake over all the world, as so many slaves, belly-gods, and land-serpents, *et totus orbis ventri nimis angustus*, the whole world cannot satisfy their appetite. 'Sea, land, rivers, lakes, etc., may not give content to their raging guts.' To make up the mess, what immoderate drinking in every place! *Senem potum pota trahebat anus* [old men, old women drunk go arm in arm], how they flock to the tavern! as if they were *fruges consumere nati*, born to no other end but to eat and drink, like Offellius Bibulus, that famous Roman parasite, *qui dum vixit, aut bibit aut minxit*; as so many casks to hold wine, yea worse than a cask, that mars wine, and itself is not marred by it, yet these are brave men, *Silenus ebrius* [drunken Silenus] was no braver. *Et quæ fuerunt vitia, mores sunt* [what once was vice is now highly moral]: 'tis now the fashion of our times, an honour: *Nunc vero res ista eo rediit* (as Chrysost., *serm.* 30 *in* 5 *Ephes.*, comments) *ut effeminatæ ridendæque ignaviæ loco habeatur, nolle inebriari*; 'tis now come to that pass that he is no gentleman, a very milksop, a clown, of no bringing-up, that will not drink; fit for no company; he is your only gallant that plays it off finest, no disparagement now to stagger in the streets, reel, rave, etc., but much to his fame and renown; as in like case Epidicus told Thesprio his fellow-servant, in the poet. *Edepol facinus improbum* [in truth, a very wrong action], one urged; the other replied, *At jam alii fecere idem, erit illi illa res honori*, 'tis now no fault, there be so many brave examples to bear one out; 'tis a credit to have a strong brain, and carry his liquor well; the sole contention who can drink most, and fox his fellow the soonest. 'Tis the *summum bonum* of our tradesmen, their felicity, life, and soul (*Tanta dulcedine affectant*, saith Pliny, *lib.* 14, *cap.* 12, *ut magna pars non aliud vitæ præmium intelligat* [strong drink gives such pleasure that manȳ people think there is nothing else worth living for]), their chief comfort, to be merry together in an alehouse or tavern, as our modern Muscovites do in their mead-inns, and Turks in their coffa-houses, which much resemble our taverns; they will labour hard all day long to be drunk at night, and spend *totius anni labores* [the earnings of a whole year], as St Ambrose adds, in a tippling feast; convert day into night, as Seneca taxes some in his times, *Pervertunt officia noctis et lucis* [they turn day into night and night into day]; when we rise, they commonly go to bed, like our antipodes:

> *Nosque ubi primus equis oriens afflavit anhelis,*
> *Illis sera rubens accendit lumina vesper.*

> [When dawn for us pants up the East on high,
> For them the eve glows in the western sky.]

So did Petronius in Tacitus, Heliogabalus in Lampridius.

> *Noctes vigilabat ad ipsum*
> *Mane, diem totum stertebat.*

> [He drank the night away
> Till rising dawn, then snor'd out all the day.]

Smindyrides the Sybarite never saw the sun rise or set so much as once in twenty years. Verres, against whom Tully so much inveighs, in winter he never was *extra tectum* [out of his house], *vix extra lectum*, never almost out of bed, still wenching and drinking; so did he spend his time, and so do myriads in our days. They have *gymnasia bibonum* [training grounds for topers], schools and rendezvous; these Centaurs and Lapithæ toss pots and bowls as so many balls; invent new tricks, as sausages, anchovies, tobacco, caviare, pickled oysters, herrings, fumadoes, etc., innumerable salt meats to increase their appetite, and study how to hurt themselves by taking antidotes 'to carry their drink the better'; 'and when naught else serves, they will go forth, or be conveyed out, to empty their gorge, that they may return to drink afresh.' They make laws, *insanos leges, contra bibendi fallacias* [crazy laws against attempts to shirk drinking], and brag of it when they have done, crowning that man that is soonest gone, as their drunken predecessors have done (*Quid ego video? Ps. Cum corona Pseudolum ebrium tuum.* [What do I see? Your friend Pseudolus, drunk and garlanded]), and when they are dead, will have a can of wine with Maron's old woman to be engraven on their tombs. So they triumph in villainy, and justify their wickedness with Rabelais, that French Lucian: drunkenness is better for the body than physic, because there be more old drunkards than old physicians. Many such frothy arguments they have, inviting and encouraging others to do as they do, and love them dearly for it (no glue like to that of good fellowship). So did Alcibiades in Greece; Nero, Bonosus, Heliogabalus in Rome, or Alegabalus rather, as he was styled of old (as Ignatius proves out of some old coins). So do many great men still, as Heresbachius observes. When a prince drinks till his eyes stare, like Bitias in the poet,

> *Ille impiger hausit*
> *Spumantem vino pateram,*

[Eager he drained the bowl, brimming with wine,]

and comes off clearly, sound trumpets, fife and drums, the spectators will applaud him, 'the bishop himself' (if he belie them not) 'with his chaplain will stand by and do as much,' *O dignum principe haustum*, 'twas done like a prince. 'Our Dutchmen invite all comers with a pail and a dish, *velut infundibula integras obbas exhauriunt, et in monstrosis poculis ipsi monstrosi monstrosius epotant* [they take in whole beakers like funnels, and swill hugely out of huge goblets], making barrels of their bellies.' *Incredible dictu*, as one of their own countrymen complains, *quantum liquoris immodestissima gens capiat* [the amount of liquor these heavy drinkers can consume is incredible], etc.; 'how they love a man that will be drunk, crown him and honour him for it, hate him that will not pledge him, stab him, kill him': a most intolerable offence, and not to be forgiven. 'He is a mortal enemy that will not drink with him,' as Munster relates of the Saxons. So in Poland, he is the best servitor, and the honestest fellow, saith Alexander Gaguinus, that drinketh most healths to the honour of his master; he shall be rewarded as a good servant, and held the bravest fellow that carries his liquor best, whenas a brewer's horse will bear much more than any sturdy drinker; yet for his noble exploits in this kind he shall be accounted a most valiant man, for *Tam inter epulas fortis vir esse potest ac in bello*, as much valour is to be found in feasting as in fighting, and some of our city captains and carpet knights will make this good, and prove it. Thus they many times wilfully pervert the good temperature of their bodies, stifle their wits, strangle nature, and degenerate into beasts.

Some again are in the other extreme, and draw this mischief on their heads by too ceremonious and strict diet, being overprecise, cockney-like, and curious in their observation of meats, times, as that *medicina statica* [regimen of diet] prescribes, just so many ounces at dinner, which Lessius enjoins, so much at supper, not a little more, nor a little less, of such meat, and at such hours, a diet-drink in the morning, cock-broth, china-broth, at dinner plum-broth, a chicken, a rabbit, rib of a rack of mutton, wing of a capon, the merry-thought of a hen, etc.; to sounder bodies this is too nice and most absurd. Others offend in over-much fasting: pining adays, saith Guianerius, and waking anights, as many Moors and Turks in these our times do. 'Anchorites, monks, and the rest of that superstitious rank' (as the same Guianerius witnesseth, that he hath often seen to have happened in his time) 'through immoderate fasting, have been frequently mad.' Of such men belike Hippocrates speaks, 1 *Aphor.* 5, whenas he saith, 'They more offend in too sparing diet, and are worse damnified, than they that feed liberally and are ready to surfeit.'

Love-Melancholy

There will not be wanting, I presume, one or other that will much discommend some part of this treatise of love-melancholy, and object (which Erasmus in his preface to Sir Thomas More suspects of his) 'that it is too light for a divine, too comical a subject' to speak of love-symptoms, too phantastical, and fit alone for a wanton poet, a feeling young lovesick gallant, an effeminate courtier, or some such idle person. And 'tis true they say: for by the naughtiness of men it is so come to pass, as Caussinus observes, *ut castis auribus vox amoris suspecta sit, et invisa,* the very name of love is odious to chaster ears; and therefore some again, out of an affected gravity, will dislike all for the name's sake before they read a word, dissembling with him in Petronius, and seem to be angry that their ears are violated with such obscene speeches, that so they may be admired 'for grave philosophers and staid carriage.' They cannot abide to hear talk of love-toys, or amorous discourses, *vultu, gestu, oculis* [in expression, gestures, glances], in their outward actions averse, and yet in their cogitations they are all out as bad, if not worse than others.

Erubuit, posuitque meum Lucretia librum,
  Sed coram Bruto; Brute recede, legit.

[When Brutus came, she blushed and hid my book;
  She 'll read again when Brutus does not look.]

But let these cavillers and counterfeit Catos know, that,
as the Lord John answered the queen in that Italian
Guazzo, an old, a grave, discreet man is fittest to discourse of love matters, because he hath likely more
experience, observed more, hath a more staid judgment,
can better discern, resolve, discuss, advise, give better
cautions and more solid precepts, better inform his audi-
tors in such a subject, and by reason of his riper years
sooner divert. Besides, *nihil in hac amoris voce subtimen-
dum*, there is nothing here to be excepted at; love is a
species of melancholy, and a necessary part of this my
treatise, which I may not omit; *operi suscepto inserviendum
fuit*: so Jacobus Micyllus pleadeth for himself in his translation of Lucian's Dialogues, and so do I; I must and will
perform my task. And that short excuse of Mercerus for
his edition of Aristænetus shall be mine: 'If I have spent
my time ill to write, let not them be so idle as to read.'
But I am persuaded it is not so ill spent, I ought not to
excuse or repent myself of this subject, on which many
grave and worthy men have written whole volumes,
Plato, Plutarch, Plotinus, Maximus Tyrius, Alcinous,
Avicenna, Leon Hebræus in three large dialogues,
Xenophon, *Sympos.*, Theophrastus, if we may believe
Athenæus, *lib. 13, cap. 9*, Picus Mirandula, Marius Æquic-
ola, both in Italian, Kornmannus, *de linea Amoris, lib. 3,*

Petrus Godefridus hath handled in three books, P. Hædus, and which almost every physician, as Arnoldus Villanovanus, Valleriola, *Observat. med. lib. 2, observ. 7*, Ælian Montaltus and Laurentius in their treatises of melancholy, Jason Pratensis, *de morb. cap.*, Valescus de Taranta, Gordonius, Hercules de Saxonia, Savonarola, Langius, etc., have treated of apart, and in their works. I excuse myself, therefore, with Peter Godefridus, Valleriola, Ficinus, and in Langius' words: 'Cadmus Milesius writ fourteen books of love, and why should I be ashamed to write an epistle in favour of young men, of this subject?' A company of stern readers dislike the second of the Æneids, and Virgil's gravity, for inserting such amorous passions in an heroical subject; but Servius, his commentator, justly vindicates the poet's worth, wisdom, and discretion in doing as he did. Castalio would not have young men read the Canticles, because to his thinking it was too light and amorous a tract, a ballad of ballads, as our old English translation hath it. He might as well forbid the reading of Genesis, because of the loves of Jacob and Rachel, the stories of Sichem and Dinah, Judah and Tamar; reject the Book of Numbers, for the fornications of the people of Israel with the Moabites; that of Judges for Samson and Dalilah's embracings; that of the Kings, for David and Bathsheba's adulteries, the incest of Amnon and Tamar, Solomon's concubines, etc., the stories of Esther, Judith, Susanna, and many such. Dicæarchus, and some other, carp at Plato's majesty, that he would vouchsafe to indite such love-toys: amongst the rest, for that dalliance with Agatho:

Suavia dans Agathoni, animam ipse in labra tenebam;
  Ægra etenim properans tanquam abitura fuit.

[When kissing Agathon, I held my very soul upon my lips,
for it rushed thither as though it meant to leave me.]

For my part, saith Maximus Tyrius, a great Platonist
himself, *me non tantum admiratio habet, sed etiam stupor*, I
do not only admire, but stand amazed to read that Plato
and Socrates both should expel Homer from their city
because he writ of such light and wanton subjects, *quod
Junonem cum Jove in Ida concumbentes inducit, ab immortali
nube contectos*, Vulcan's net, Mars' and Venus' fopperies
before all the gods; because Apollo fled when he was
persecuted by Achilles, the gods were wounded and ran
whining away, as Mars that roared louder than Stentor,
and covered nine acres of ground with his fall; Vulcan
was a summer's day falling down from heaven, and in
Lemnos Isle brake his leg, etc., with such ridiculous
passages; whenas both Socrates and Plato, by his testimony, writ lighter themselves: *Quid enim tam distat* (as he
follows it) *quam amans a temperante, formarum admirator a
demente?* [What greater contrast can there be than
between a lover and a man of self-restraint, an admirer
of beauty and a madman?], what can be more absurd
than for grave philosophers to treat of such fooleries, to
admire Autolycus, Alcibiades, for their beauties as they
did, to run after, to gaze, to dote on fair Phædrus,
delicate Agatho, young Lysis, fine Charmides, *hæccine
philosophum decent?* Doth this become grave philosophers? Thus peradventure Callias, Thrasymachus,

Polus, Aristophanes, or some of his adversaries and emu-
lators might object; but neither they nor Anytus and
Meletus, his bitter enemies, that condemned him for
teaching Critias to tyrannize, his impiety for swearing
by dogs and plane-trees, for his juggling sophistry, etc.,
never so much as upbraided him with impure love,
writing or speaking of that subject; and therefore without
question, as he concludes, both Socrates and Plato in this
are justly to be excused. But suppose they had been a
little overseen, should divine Plato be defamed? No;
rather, as he said of Cato's drunkenness, if Cato were
drunk, it should be no vice at all to be drunk. They
reprove Plato then, but without cause (as Ficinus pleads);
'for all love is honest and good, and they are worthy to
be loved that speak well of love.' 'Being to speak of this
admirable affection of love' (saith Valleriola), 'there lies
open a vast and philosophical field to my discourse, by
which many lovers become mad: let me leave my more
serious meditations, wander in these philosophical fields,
and look into those pleasant groves of the Muses, where
with unspeakable variety of flowers we may make gar-
lands to ourselves, not to adorn us only, but with their
pleasant smell and juice to nourish our souls, and fill our
minds desirous of knowledge,' etc. After a harsh and
unpleasing discourse of melancholy, which hath hitherto
molested your patience and tired the author, give him
leave with Godefridus the lawyer, and Laurentius, to
recreate himself in this kind after his laborious studies,
'since so many grave divines and worthy men have
without offence to manners, to help themselves and
others, voluntarily written of it.' Heliodorus, a bishop,

penned a love story of Theagenes and Chariclea, and when some Catos of his time reprehended him for it, chose rather, saith Nicephorus, to leave his bishopric than his book. Æneas Sylvius, an ancient divine, and past forty years of age, as he confesseth himself (after Pope Pius Secundus), indited that wanton history of Euryalus and Lucretia. And how many superintendents of learning could I reckon up, that have written of light phantastical subjects! Beroaldus, Erasmus; Alpheratius, twenty-four times printed in Spanish, etc. Give me leave then to refresh my Muse a little, and my weary readers, to expatiate in this delightsome field, *hoc deliciarum campo*, as Fonseca terms it, to season a surly discourse with a more pleasing aspersion of love matters. *Edulcare vitam convenit*, as the poet invites us, *curas nugis*, etc., 'tis good to sweeten our life with some pleasing toys to relish it, and, as Pliny tells us, *magna pars studiosorum amœnitates quærimus*, most of our students love such pleasant subjects. Though Macrobius teach us otherwise, 'that those old sages banished all such light tracts from their studies to nurses' cradles, to please only the ear'; yet out of Apuleius I will oppose as honourable patrons, Solon, Plato, Xenophon, Hadrian, etc., that as highly approve of these treatises. On the other side methinks they are not to be disliked, they are not so unfit. I will not peremptorily say, as one did, *tam suavia dicam facinora, ut male sit ei qui talibus non delectetur*, I will tell you such pretty stories, that foul befall him that is not pleased with them; *neque dicam ea quæ vobis usui sit audivisse, et voluptati meminisse* [nor will I say things which you will hear with profit and remember with pleasure], with that confidence

as Beroaldus doth his enarrations on Propertius. I will
not expect or hope for that approbation which Lipsius
gives to his Epictetus: *Pluris facio quum relego; semper ut
novum, et quum repetivi, repetendum,* the more I read, the
more shall I covet to read. I will not press you with my
pamphlets, or beg attention, but if you like them you
may. Pliny holds it expedient, and most fit, *severitatem
jucunditate etiam in scriptis condire,* to season our works
with some pleasant discourse; Synesius approves it, *licet
in ludicris ludere* [it is permissible to trifle with trifles]; the
poet admires it:

> *Omne tulit punctum qui miscuit utile dulci;*

> [All votes to him the first place shall assign
> Who with the sweet the useful can combine;]

and there be those, without question, that are more
willing to read such toys than I am to write. 'Let me not
live,' saith Aretine's Antonia, 'if I had not rather hear thy
discourse than see a play!' No doubt but there be more
of her mind, ever have been, ever will be, as Hierome
bears me witness: 'A far greater part had rather read
Apuleius than Plato.' Tully himself confesseth he could
not understand Plato's *Timæus,* and therefore cared less
for it; but every schoolboy hath that famous testament
of Grunnius Corocotta Porcellus at his fingers' ends. The
comical poet

> *Id sibi negoti credidit solum dari,*
> *Populo ut placerent quas fecisset fabulas,*

made this his only care and sole study, to please the people, tickle the ear, and to delight; but mine earnest intent is as much to profit as to please, *non tam ut populo placerem, quam ut populum juvarem*; and these my writings, I hope, shall take like gilded pills, which are so composed as well to tempt the appetite and deceive the palate, as to help and medicinally work upon the whole body; my lines shall not only recreate but rectify the mind. I think I have said enough; if not, let him that is otherwise minded remember that of Madaurensis; 'he was in his life a philosopher' (as Ausonius apologizeth for him), 'in his epigrams a lover, in his precepts most severe; in his epistle to Cærellia a wanton.' Annianus, Sulpicius, Evenus, Menander, and many old poets besides, did *in scriptis prurire*, write Fescennines, Atellanes, and lascivious songs, *lætam materiam*; yet they had *in moribus censuram et severitatem*, they were chaste, severe, and upright livers.

> *Castum esse decet pium poetam*
> *Ipsum, versiculos nihil necesse est,*
> *Qui tum denique habent salem et leporem.*

> ['Tis true, the poet should be chaste;
> But need his lines, so they be graced
> With wit, and captivate the taste?]

I am of Catullus' opinion, and make the same apology in mine own behalf: *Hoc etiam quod scribo, pendet plerumque ex aliorum sententia et auctoritate; nec ipse forsan insanio, sed insanientes sequor. Atqui detur hoc insanire me; semel insanivimus omnes, et tute ipse opinor insanis aliquando, et is, et ille, et ego scilicet* [I write for the most part to satisfy the taste and judgment of others; I am not mad myself, but I follow those who are. Yet grant that this shows me mad; we have all raved once, and you yourself, I think, dote sometimes, and he, and he, and of course I too]. *Homo sum, humani a me nihil alienum puto* [I am a human being, I count nothing human foreign to myself]: and, which he urgeth for himself, accused of the like fault, I as justly plead, *Lasciva est nobis pagina, vita proba est*; howsoever my lines err, my life is honest, *Vita verecunda est, musa jocosa mihi*. But I presume I need no such apologies; I need not, as Socrates in Plato, cover his face when he spake of love, or blush and hide mine eyes, as Pallas did in her hood, when she was consulted by Jupiter about Mercury's marriage, *quod super nuptiis virgo consulitur*; it is no such lascivious, obscene, or wanton discourse; I have not offended your chaster ears with anything that is here written, as many French and Italian authors in their modern language of late have done, nay, some of our Latin pontificial writers, Zanchius, Asorius, Abulensis, Burchardus, etc., whom Rivet accuseth to be more lascivious than Virgil in *Priapeiis*, Petronius in *Catalectis*, Aristophanes in *Lysistrata*, Martialis, or any other pagan profane writer, *qui tam atrociter* (one notes) *hoc genere peccarunt, ut multa ingeniosissime scripta obscœnitatum gratia castœ mentes abhorreant* [who have erred so grossly in this sort that much of their most ingenious writing repels pure minds by its obscenity]. 'Tis not scurrile this, but chaste, honest, most part serious, and even of religion itself. 'Incensed' (as he said) 'with the love of finding love, we have sought it, and found it.' More yet, I have augmented and added something to this light treatise (if light) which was not in the former editions, I am not ashamed to confess it, with a good author, *quod extendi et locupletari hoc subjectum plerique postulabant, et eorum importunitate victus, animum utcunque renitentem eo adegi, ut jam sexta vice calamum in manum sumerem, scriptionique longe et a studiis et professione mea alienæ me accingerem, horas aliquas a seriis meis occupationibus interim suffuratus, easque veluti ludo cuidam ac recreationi destinans* [yielding to the solicitations of many who begged me to dwell at greater length on this topic, I overcame my reluctance and for the sixth time took the pen in my hand for a kind of composition very foreign to my studies and profession, stealing from my serious occupations a few hours to devote to lighter pursuits]:

> *Cogor . . . retrorsum*
> *Vela dare, atque iterare cursus*
> *Olim relictos,*

[I am compelled to reverse my direction and retrace my course,]

etsi non ignorarem novos fortasse detractores novis hisce interpolationibus meis minime defuturos [although well aware that these additions would procure me fresh detractors].

And thus much I have thought good to say by way of preface, lest any man (which Godefridus feared in his book) should blame in me lightness, wantonness, rashness, in speaking of love's causes, enticements, symptoms, remedies, lawful and unlawful loves, and lust itself. 'I speak it only to tax and deter others from it, not to teach, but to show the vanities and fopperies of this heroical or herculean love,' and to 'apply remedies unto it.' I will treat of this with like liberty as of the rest.

> *Sed dicam vobis, vos porro dicite multis*
> *Millibus, et facite hæc charta loquatur anus.*

> [I will tell you, and do you go and tell thousands more,
>   so that this page shall chatter like an old woman.]

Condemn me not, good reader, then, or censure me hardly, if some part of this treatise to thy thinking as yet be too light; but consider better of it. *Omnia munda mundis* [to the pure all things are pure], a naked man to a modest woman is no otherwise than a picture, as Augusta Livia truly said, and *mala mens, malus animus* [to construe it ill shows an evil will], 'tis as 'tis taken. If in thy censure it be too light, I advise thee as Lipsius did his reader for some places of Plautus, *Istos quasi Sirenum scopulos prætervehare* [to pass them by like rocks of the Sirens], if they like thee not, let them pass; or oppose that which is good to that which is bad, and reject not therefore all. For to invert that verse of Martial, and with Hierome Wolfius to apply it to my present purpose, *sunt mala, sunt quædam mediocria, sunt bona plura*; some is good, some bad, some is indifferent. I say farther with him yet, I have inserted (*levicula quædam et ridicula ascribere non sum gravatus, circumforanea quædam e theatris, a plateis, etiame e popinis* [I have not refrained from putting down certain levities and absurdities, such as are current in the theatres, the market-places, and even the cook-shops]) some things more homely, light, or comical, *litans Gratiis* [sacrificing to the Graces], etc., which I would request every man to interpret to the best, and, as Julius Cæsar Scaliger besought Cardan, *Si quid urbaniuscule lusum a nobis, per deos immortales te oro, Hieronyme Cardane, ne me male capias* [if I have written anything in lighter vein, please do not take it amiss], I beseech thee, good reader, not to mistake me, or misconstrue what is here written; *per Musas et Charites, et omnia poetarum numina, benigne lector, oro te ne me male capias.* 'Tis a comical subject; in sober sadness I crave pardon of what is amiss, and desire thee to suspend thy judgment, wink at small faults, or to be silent at least; but if thou likest, speak well of it, and wish me good success. *Extremum hunc, Arethusa, mihi concede laborem* [grant me, Arethusa, to achieve this last labour].

I am resolved howsoever, *velis, nolis, audacter stadium intrare,* [whether thou wilt or not, to enter the arena boldly], in the Olympics, with those Eliensian wrestlers in Philostratus, boldly to show myself in this common stage, and in this tragi-comedy of love to act several parts, some satirically, some comically, some in a mixed tone, as the subject I have in hand gives occasion, and present scene shall required or offer itself.

Love's Beginning, Object, Definition, Division

'Love's limits are ample and great, and a spacious walk
it hath, beset with thorns,' and for that cause, which
Scaliger reprehends in Cardan, 'not lightly to be passed
over.' Lest I incur the same censure, I will examine
all the kinds of love, his nature, beginning, difference,
objects, how it is honest or dishonest, a virtue or vice, a
natural passion or a disease, his power and effects, how
far it extends: of which, although something has been
said in the first partition, in those sections of perturbations ('for love and hatred are the first and most
common passions, from which all the rest arise, and are
attendant,' as Piccolomineus holds, or, as Nich. Caussinus, the *primum mobile* [first mover] of all other affections, which carry them all about them), I will now
more copiously dilate, through all his parts and several
branches, that so it may better appear what love is, and
how it varies with the objects, how in defect, or (which is
most ordinary and common) immoderate and in excess,
causeth melancholy.

Love, universally taken, is defined to be a desire, as a
word of more ample signification; and though Leon
Hebræus, the most copious writer of this subject, in his
third dialogue makes no difference, yet in his first he
distinguisheth them again, and defines love by desire.
'Love is a voluntary affection, and desire to enjoy that

which is good. Desire wisheth, love enjoys; the end of
the one is the beginning of the other; that which we love
is present; that which we desire is absent.' 'It is worth
the labour,' saith Plotinus, 'to consider well of love,
whether it be a god or a devil, or passion of the mind,
or partly god, partly devil, partly passion.' He concludes
love to participate of all three, to arise from desire of
that which is beautiful and fair, and defines it to be 'an
action of the mind desiring that which is good.' Plato
calls it the great devil, for its vehemency, and sovereignty
over all other passions, and defines it an appetite 'by
which we desire some good to be present.' Ficinus in his
comment adds the word fair to this definition: 'Love is
a desire of enjoying that which is good and fair.' Austin
dilates this common definition, and will have love to be
a delectation of the heart, 'for something which we seek
to win, or joy to have, coveting by desire, resting in joy.'
Scaliger, *Exerc.* 301, taxeth these former definitions, and
will not have love to be defined by desire or appetite;
'for when we enjoy the things we desire, there remains
no more appetite': as he defines it, 'Love is an affection
by which we are either united to the things we love, or
perpetuate our union'; which agrees in part with Leon
Hebræus.

Now this love varies as his object varies, which is
always good, amiable, fair, gracious, and pleasant. 'All
things desire that which is good,' as we are taught in the
Ethics, or at least that which to them seems to be good;
quid enim vis mali (as Austin well infers), *dic mihi? puto*
nihil in omnibus actionibus; thou wilt wish no harm, I
suppose, no ill in all thine actions, thoughts, or desires,

nihil mali vis; thou wilt not have bad corn, bad soil, a naughty tree, but all good: a good servant, a good horse, a good son, a good friend, a good neighbour, a good wife. From this goodness comes beauty; from beauty, grace and comeliness, which result as so many rays from their good parts, make us to love, and so to covet it: for were it not pleasing and gracious in our eyes, we should not seek. 'No man loves,' saith Aristotle, 9 *Mor. cap.* 5, 'but he that was first delighted with comeliness and beauty.' As this fair object varies, so doth our love; for, as Proclus holds, *omne pulchrum amabile*, every fair thing is amiable, and what we love is fair and gracious in our eyes, or at least we do so apprehend and still esteem of it. 'Amiableness is the object of love, the scope and end is to obtain it, for whose sake we love, and which our mind covets to enjoy.' And it seems to us especially fair and good; for good, fair, and unity cannot be separated. Beauty shines, Plato saith, and by reason of its splendour and shining causeth admiration; and the fairer the object is, the more eagerly it is sought. For, as the same Plato defines it, 'Beauty is a lively shining or glittering brightness, resulting from effused good by ideas, seeds, reasons, shadows, stirring up our minds that by this good they may be united and made one.' Others will have beauty to be the perfection of the whole composition, 'caused out of the congruous symmetry, measure, order and manner of parts; and that comeliness which proceeds from this beauty is called grace, and from thence all fair things are gracious.' For grace and beauty are so wonderfully annexed, 'so sweetly and gently win our souls, and strongly allure, that they confound our judgment and cannot be distinguished. Beauty and grace are like those beams and shinings that come from the glorious and divine sun,' which are diverse, as they proceed from the diverse objects, to please and affect our several senses; as 'the species of beauty are taken at our eyes, ears, or conceived in our inner soul,' as Plato disputes at large in his dialogue *de Pulchro, Phædrus, Hippias*, and, after many sophistical errors confuted, concludes that beauty is a grace in all things, delighting the eyes, ears, and soul itself; so that, as Valesius infers hence, whatsoever pleaseth our ears, eyes, and soul, must needs be beautiful, fair, and delightsome to us. 'And nothing can more please our ears than music, or pacify our minds.' Fair houses, pictures, orchards, gardens, fields, a fair hawk, a fair horse is most acceptable unto us; whatsoever pleaseth our eyes and ears, we call beautiful and fair; 'Pleasure belongeth to the rest of the senses, but grace and beauty to these two alone.' As the objects vary and are diverse, so they diversely affect our eyes, ears, and soul itself; which gives occasion to some to make so many several kinds of love as there be objects: one beauty ariseth from God, of which and divine love St Dionysius, with many Fathers and neoterics, have written just volumes, *de amore dei* [concerning the love of God], as they term it, many parænetical discourses; another from His creatures: there is a beauty of the body, a beauty of the soul, a beauty from virtue, *formam martyrum* [a beauty of martyrs], Austin calls it, *quam videmus oculis animi*, which we see with the eyes of our mind; which beauty, as Tully saith, if we could discern with these corporal eyes, *admirabiles sui amores excitaret,* would cause admirable affections, and ravish our souls. This other beauty, which ariseth from those extreme parts, and graces which proceed from gestures, speeches, several motions, and proportions of creatures, men and women (especially from women, which made those old poets put the three Graces still in Venus' company, as attending on her and holding up her train), are infinite almost, and vary their names with their objects, as love of money, covetousness, love of beauty, lust, immoderate desire of any pleasure, concupiscence, friendship, love, good will, etc., and is either virtue or vice, honest, dishonest, in excess, defect, as shall be showed in his place; heroical love, religious love, etc., which may be reduced to a twofold division, according to the principal parts which are affected, the brain and liver: *amor et amicitia* [love and friendship], which Scaliger, *Exercitat.* 301, Valesius, and Melancthon warrant out of Plato, φιλεῖν and ἐρᾶν, from that speech of Pausanias, belike, that makes two Veneres and two loves. 'One Venus is ancient without a mother, and descended from heaven, whom we call celestial; the younger, begotten of Jupiter and Dione, whom commonly we call Venus.' Ficinus, in his comment upon this place, *cap.* 8, following Plato, calls these two devils, or good and bad angels according to us, which are still hovering about our souls. 'The one rears to heaven, the other depresseth us to hell; the one good, which stirs us up to the contemplation of that divine beauty for whose sake we perform justice and all godly offices, study philosophy, etc.; the other base, and though bad yet to be respected; for indeed both are good in their own natures: procreation of children is as

necessary as that finding out of truth, but therefore called
bad, because it is abused, and withdraws our soul from
the speculation of that other to viler objects.' So far
Ficinus. St Austin, *lib.* 15 *de Civ. Dei, et sup. Ps. lxiv*, hath
delivered as much in effect: 'Every creature is good, and
may be loved well or ill': and 'Two cities make two
loves, Jerusalem and Babylon, the love of God the one,
the love of the world the other; of these two cities we
all are citizens, as by examination of ourselves we may
soon find, and of which.' The one love is the root of all
mischief, the other of all good. So, in his 15th *cap. lib. de
amor. Ecclesiæ*, he will have those four cardinal virtues to
be naught else but love rightly composed; in his 15th
book *de Civ. Dei, cap.* 22, he calls virtue the order of love,
whom Thomas following, 1, *part.* 2, *quæst.* 55, *art.* 1, and
quæst. 56, 3, *quæst.* 62, *art.* 2, confirms as much, and
amplifies in many words. Lucian, to the same purpose,
hath a division of his own: 'One love was born in the
sea, which is as various and raging in young men's breasts
as the sea itself, and causeth burning lust: the other is
that golden chain which was let down from heaven, and
with a divine fury ravisheth our souls, made to the image
of God, and stirs us up to comprehend the innate and
incorruptible beauty to which we were once created.'
Beroaldus hath expressed all this in an epigram of his:

> *Dogmata divini memorant si vera Platonis,*
> *Sunt geminæ Veneres, et geminatus amor.*
> *Cælestis Venus est nullo generata parente,*
> *Quæ casto sanctos nectit amore viros.*
> *Altera sed Venus est totum vulgata per orbem,*

Quæ divum mentes alligat, atque hominum;
Improba, seductrix, petulans, etc.

If divine Plato's tenents they be true,
    Two Veneres, two loves there be;
The one from heaven, unbegotten still,
    Which knits our souls in unity.
The other famous over all the world,
    Binding the hearts of gods and men;
Dishonest, wanton, and seducing she,
    Rules whom she will, both where and when.

This twofold division of love Origen likewise follows, in his Comment on the Canticles, one from God, the other from the devil, as he holds (understanding it in the worse sense), which many others repeat and imitate. Both which (to omit all subdivisions) in excess or defect, as they are abused, or degenerate, cause melancholy in a particular kind, as shall be showed in his place. Austin, in another tract, makes a threefold division of this love, which we may use well or ill: 'God, our neighbour, and the world: God above us, our neighbour next us, the world beneath us. In the course of our desires, God hath three things, the world one, our neighbour two. Our desire to God is either from God, with God, or to God, and ordinarily so runs. From God, when it receives from Him, whence, and for which it should love Him: with God, when it contradicts His will in nothing: to God, when it seeks to repose and rest itself in Him. Our love to our neighbour may proceed from him, and run with him, not to him: from him, as when we rejoice of his good safety and well doing: with him, when we desire to have him a fellow and companion of our journey in the way of the Lord: not in him, because there is no aid, hope, or confidence in man. From the world our love comes, when we begin to admire the Creator in His works, and glorify God in His creatures: with the world it should run, if, according to the mutability of all temporalities, it should be dejected in adversity, or over-elevated in prosperity: to the world, if it would settle itself in his vain delights and studies.' Many such partitions of love I could repeat, and subdivisions, but lest (which Scaliger objects to Cardan, *Exercitat.* 501) 'I confound filthy burning lust with pure and divine love,' I will follow that accurate division of Leon Hebræus, *dial.* 2, betwixt Sophia and Philo, where he speaks of natural, sensible, and rational love, and handleth each apart. Natural love or hatred is that sympathy or antipathy which is to be seen in animate and inanimate creatures, in the four elements, metals, stones, *gravia tendunt deorsum* [heavy bodies tend downwards], as a stone to his centre, fire upward, and rivers to the sea. The sun, moon, and stars go still round, *amantes naturæ debita exercere*, for love of perfection. This love is manifest, I say, in inanimate creatures. How comes a loadstone to draw iron to it? jet chaff? the ground to covet showers, but for love? No creature, St Hierome concludes, is to be found, *quod non aliquid amat* [that doth not love something], no stock, no stone, that hath not some feeling of love. 'Tis more eminent in plants, herbs, and is especially observed in vegetals; as between the vine and elm a great sympathy; between the vine and the cabbage, between the vine and the olive (*Virgo fugit Bromium* [the virgin shuns Bacchus]), between the vine and bays a great antipathy; 'the vine loves not the bay, nor his smell, and will kill him, if he grow near him'; the bur and the lentil cannot endure one another, the olive and the myrtle embrace each other in roots and branches if they grow near. Read more of this in Piccolomineus, *grad. 7, cap.* 1; Crescentius, *lib. 5 de agric.*; Baptista Porta, *de mag. lib.* 1, *cap. de plant. odio et element. sym.*; Fracastorius *de sym. et antip.* Of the love and hatred of planets, consult with every astrologer: Leon Hebræus gives many fabulous reasons, and moralizeth them withal.

Sensible love is that of brute beasts, of which the same Leon Hebræus, *dial.* 2, assigns these causes. First, for the pleasure they take in the act of generation, male and female love one another. Secondly, for the preservation of the species, and desire of young brood. Thirdly, for the mutual agreement, as being of the same kind: *Sus sui, canis cani, bos bovi, et asinus asino pulcherrimus videtur* [pig appears most beautiful to pig, ass to ass, ox to ox, dog to dog], as Epicharmus held, and according to that adage of Diogenianus, *Adsidet usque graculus apud graculum* [one daw sits by another], they much delight in one another's company, *Formicæ grata est formica, cicada cicadæ* [ant likes ant and grasshopper grasshopper], and birds of a feather will gather together. Fourthly, for custom, use, and familiarity, as if a dog be trained up with a lion and a bear, contrary to their natures, they will love each other. Hawks, dogs, horses, love their masters and keepers: many stories I could relate in this kind, but see Gillius, *de hist. anim. lib.* 3, *cap.* 14, those two Epistles of Lipsius, of dogs and horses, A. Gellius, etc. Fifthly, for bringing up, as if a bitch bring up a kid, a hen ducklings, an hedge-sparrow a cuckoo, etc.

The third kind is *amor cognitionis*, as Leon calls it, rational love, *intellectivus amor*, and is proper to men, on which I must insist. This appears in God, angels, men. God is love itself, the fountain of love, the disciple of love, as Plato styles Him; the servant of peace, the God of love and peace; have peace with all men and God is with you.

> *Quisquis veneratur Olympum,*
> *Ipse sibi mundum subjicit atque Deum.*

[Whoever reveres heaven subjects to himself the world and God.]

'By this love' (saith Gerson) 'we purchase heaven,' and buy the kingdom of God. This love is either in the Trinity itself (for the Holy Ghost is the love of the Father and the Son, etc., John iii, 35, and v, 20, and xiv, 31), or towards us His creatures, as in making the world. *Amor mundum fecit*, love built cities, *mundi anima* [the soul of the world], invented arts, sciences, and all good things, incites us to virtue and humanity, combines and quickens; keeps peace on earth, quietness by sea, mirth in the winds and elements, expels all fear, anger, and rusticity; *circulus a bono in bonum*, a round circle still from good to good; for love is the beginner and end of all our actions, the efficient and instrumental cause, as our poets in their symbols, impresses, emblems of rings, squares, etc., shadow unto us.

Si rerum quæris fuerit quis finis et ortus,
Desine; nam causa est unica solus amor.

If first and last of anything you wit,
Cease; love's the sole and only cause of it.

Love, saith Leo, made the world, and afterwards, in redeeming of it, 'God so loved the world, that he gave his only begotten son for it' (John iii, 16), 'Behold what love the Father hath showed on us, that we should be called the sons of God' (1 John iii, 1). Or by His sweet Providence, in protecting of it; either all in general, or His saints elect and Church in particular, whom He keeps as the apple of His eye, whom He loves freely, as Hosea, xiv; 5, speaks, and dearly respects, *Carior est ipsis homo quam sibi* [man is dearer to them than to himself]. Not that we are fair, nor for any merit or grace of ours, for we are most vile and base; but out of His incomparable love and goodness, out of His Divine Nature. And this is that Homer's golden chain, which reacheth down from heaven to earth, by which every creature is annexed, and depends on his Creator. He made all, saith Moses, 'and it was good,' and He loves it as good.

The love of angels and living souls is mutual amongst themselves, towards us militant in the Church, and all such as love God; as the sunbeams irradiate the earth from those celestial thrones, they by their well-wishes reflect on us, *in salute hominum promovenda alacres, et constantes administri* [they are alert to promote the salvation of men, and are their constant supports], there is joy in heaven for every sinner that repenteth; they pray for us, are solicitous for our good, *casti genii* [pure guardian angels].

> *Ubi regnat caritas, suave desiderium,*
> *Lætitiaque e' amor Deo conjunctus.*

[Where reigneth charity, sweet desire, joy, and love that unites with God.]

Love proper to mortal men is the third member of this subdivision, and the subject of my following discourse.

Causes of Love-Melancholy, Sight, Beauty from the Face, Eyes, other Parts, and how it Pierceth

Many such causes may be reckoned up, but they cannot avail, except opportunity be offered of time, place, and those other beautiful objects, or artificial enticements, as kissing, conference, discourse, gestures, concur, with such-like lascivious provocations. Kornmannus, in his book *de linea amoris*, makes five degrees of lust, out of Lucian belike, which he handles in five chapters, *Visus, Colloquium, Convictus, Oscula, Tactus* [sight, converse, companionship, kissing, touch]. Sight, of all other, is the first step of this unruly love, though sometimes it be prevented by relation or hearing, or rather incensed. For there be those so apt, credulous, and facile to love, that if they hear of a proper man, or woman, they are in love before they see them, and that merely by relation, as Achilles Tatius observes. 'Such is their intemperance and lust, that they are as much maimed by report as if they saw them. Callisthenes, a rich young gentleman of Byzance in Thrace, hearing of Leucippe, Sostratus' fair daughter, was far in love with her, and, out of fame and common rumour, so much incensed, that he would needs have her to be his wife.' And sometimes by reading they are so affected, as he in Lucian confesseth of himself, 'I never read that place of Panthea in Xenophon, but I am as much affected as if I were present with her.' Such persons commonly feign a kind of beauty to themselves; and so did those three gentlewomen in Balthasar Castilio fall in love with a young man whom they never knew, but only heard him commended: or by reading of a letter; for there is a grace cometh from hearing, as a moral philosopher informeth us, 'as well from sight; and the species of love are received into the phantasy by relation alone': *ut cupere ab aspectu, sic velle ab auditu*, both senses affect. *Interdum et absentes amamus*, sometimes we love those that are absent, saith Philostratus, and gives instance in his friend Athenorodus, that loved a maid at Corinth whom he never saw; *non oculi sed mens videt*, we see with the eyes of our understanding.

But the most familiar and usual cause of love is that which comes by sight, which conveys those admirable rays of beauty and pleasing graces to the heart. Plotinus derives love from sight, ἔρως quasi ὅρασις. *Si nescis, oculi sunt in amore duces*, the eyes are the harbingers of love, and the first step of love is sight, as Lilius Giraldus proves at large, *Hist. deor. syntag.* 13; they as two sluices let in the influences of that divine, powerful, soul-ravishing, and captivating beauty, which, as one saith, 'is sharper than any dart or needle, wounds deeper into the heart; and opens a gap through our ears to that lovely wound, which pierceth the soul itself.' 'Through it love is kindled like a fire' (Ecclus. ix, 8). This amazing, confounding, admirable, amiable beauty, 'than which in all nature's treasure' (saith Isocrates) 'there is nothing so majestical and sacred, nothing so divine, lovely, precious,' 'tis nature's crown, gold and glory; *bonum si non summum, de summis tamen non infrequenter triumphans* [if it is not the highest good, it yet frequently triumphs over the highest], whose power hence may be discerned: we contemn and abhor generally such things as are foul and ugly to behold, account them filthy, but love and covet that which is fair. 'Tis beauty in all things which pleaseth and allureth us, a fair hawk, a fine garment, a goodly building, a fair house, etc. That Persian Xerxes, when he destroyed all those temples of the gods in Greece, caused that of Diana *in integrum servari*, to be spared alone for that excellent beauty and magnificence of it. Inanimate beauty can so command. 'Tis that which painters, artificers, orators, all aim at, as Erixymachus, the physician in Plato, contends. 'It was beauty first that ministered occasion to art, to find out the knowledge of carving, painting, building, to find out models, perspectives, rich furnitures, and so many rare inventions.' Whiteness in the lily, red in the rose, purple in the violet, a lustre in all things without life, the clear light of the moon, the bright beams of the sun, splendour of gold, purple, sparkling diamond, the excellent feature of the horse, the majesty of the lion, the colour of birds, peacocks' tails, the silver scales of fish, we behold with singular delight and admiration. 'And [that] which is rich in plants, delightful in flowers, wonderful in beasts, but most glorious in men,' doth make us affect and earnestly desire it, as when we hear any sweet harmony, an eloquent tongue, see any excellent quality, curious work of man, elaborate art, or aught that is exquisite, there ariseth instantly in us a longing for the same. We love such men, but most part for comeliness of person; we call them gods and goddesses, divine, serene, happy, etc.

And of all mortal men they alone (Calcagninus holds) are free from calumny; *qui divitiis, magistratu et gloria florent, injuria lacessimus*, we backbite, wrong, hate renowned, rich, and happy men, we repine at their felicity, they are undeserving, we think, fortune is a stepmother to us, a parent to them. 'We envy' (saith Isocrates) 'wise, just, honest men, except with mutual offices and kindnesses, some good turn or other, they extort this love from us; only fair persons we love at first sight, desire their acquaintance, and adore them as so many gods: we had rather serve them than command others, and account ourselves the more beholding to them, the more service they enjoin us,' though they be otherwise vicious, unhonest; we love them, favour them, and are ready to do them any good office for their beauty's sake, though they have no other good quality beside. *Dic igitur, o formose adolescens* (as that eloquent Phavorinus breaks out in Stobæus), *dic, Autolyce, suavius nectare loqueris; dic, o Telemache, vehementius Ulysse dicis; dic, Alcibiades, utcunque ebrius, libentius tibi licet ebrio auscultabimus.* 'Speak, fair youth, speak, Autolycus, thy words are sweeter than nectar; speak, O Telemachus, thou art more powerful than Ulysses; speak, Alcibiades, though drunk, we will willingly hear thee as thou art.' Faults in such are no faults: for when the said Alcibiades had stolen Anytus his gold and silver plate, he was so far from prosecuting so foul a fact (though every man else condemned his impudence and insolency) that he wished it had been more, and much better (he loved him dearly) for his sweet sake. No worth is eminent in such lovely persons, all imperfections hid; *non enim facile de his quos plurimum diligimus, turpitudinem suspicamur* [we do not readily suspect baseness in those whom we love], for hearing, sight, touch, etc., our mind and all our senses are captivated, *omnes sensus formosus delectat*. Many men have been preferred for their person alone, chosen kings, as amongst the Indians, Persians, Ethiopians of old the properest man of person the country could afford was elected their sovereign lord: *Gratior est pulchro veniens e corpore virtus* [worth pleases more in a fair bearer]; and so have many other nations thought and done, as Curtius observes; *ingens enim in corporis majestate veneratio est*, for there is a majestical presence in such men; and so far was beauty adored amongst them, that no man was thought fit to reign that was not in all parts complete and supereminent. Agis, King of Lacedæmon, had like to have been deposed, because he married a little wife; they would not have their royal issue degenerate. Who would ever have thought that Adrian the Fourth, an English monk's bastard (as Papirius Massovius writes in his life), *inops a suis relictus, squalidus et miser*, a poor forsaken child, should ever come to be Pope of Rome? But why was it? *Erat acri ingenio, facundia expedita, eleganti corpore, facieque læta ac hilari* (as he follows it out of Nubrigensis, for he ploughs with his heifer), he was wise, learned, eloquent, of a pleasant, a promising countenance, a goodly, proper man; he had, in a word, a winning look of his own, and that carried it, for that he was especially advanced. So 'Saul was a goodly person and a fair.' Maximinus elected emperor, etc. Branchus, the son of Apollo, whom he begot of Jance, Succron's daughter (saith Lactantius), when he kept King Admetus' herds in

Thessaly, now grown a man, was an earnest suitor to his mother to know his father; the nymph denied him, because Apollo had conjured her to the contrary; yet overcome by his importunity at last she sent him to his father; when he came into Apollo's presence, *malas dei reverenter osculatus* [having reverently kissed the cheeks of the god], he carried himself so well, and was so fair a young man, that Apollo was infinitely taken with the beauty of his person, he could scarce look off him, and said he was worthy of such parents, gave him a crown of gold, the spirit of divination, and in conclusion made him a demigod. *O vis superba formæ!* [What proud strength is in beauty!], a goddess beauty is, whom the very gods adore, *nam pulchros dii amant*; she is *amoris domina* [love's mistress], love's harbinger, love's loadstone, a witch, a charm, etc. Beauty is a dower of itself, a sufficient patrimony, an ample commendation, an accurate epistle, as Lucian, Apuleius, Tiraquellus, and some others conclude. *Imperio digna forma*, beauty deserves a kingdom, saith Abulensis, *Paradox. 2, cap.* 110, immortality; and 'more have got this honour and eternity for their beauty, than for all other virtues besides': and such as are fair 'are worthy to be honoured of God and men.' That Idalian Ganymede was therefore fetched by Jupiter into heaven. Hephæstion dear to Alexander, Antinous to Hadrian. Plato calls beauty for that cause a privilege of nature, *naturæ gaudentis opus*, nature's masterpiece, a dumb comment; Theophrastus, a silent fraud; still rhetoric, Carneades, that persuades without speech, a kingdom without a guard, because beautiful persons command as so many captains; Socrates, a

tyranny, 'which tyrannizeth over tyrants themselves';
which made Diogenes belike call proper women queens,
quod facerent homines quæ præciperent, because men were
so obedient to their commands. They will adore, cringe,
compliment, and bow to a common wench (if she be
fair) as if she were a noblewoman, a countess, a queen,
or a goddess. Those intemperate young men of Greece
erected at Delphi a golden image with infinite cost, to
the eternal memory of Phryne the courtesan, as Ælian
relates, for she was a most beautiful woman, insomuch,
saith Athenæus, that Apelles and Praxiteles drew Venus'
picture from her. Thus young men will adore and honour
beauty; nay kings themselves I say will do it, and voluntarily submit their sovereignty to a lovely woman. 'Wine
is strong, kings are strong, but a woman strongest'
(1 Esdras iii, 10), as Zorobabel proved at large to King
Darius, his princes and noblemen. 'Kings sit still and
command sea and land, etc., all pay tribute to the king;
but women make kings pay tribute, and have dominion
over them. When they have got gold and silver, they
submit all to a beautiful woman, give themselves wholly
to her, gape and gaze on her, and all men desire her
more than gold or silver, or any precious thing: they will
leave father and mother, and venture their lives for her,
labour and travel to get, and bring all their gains to
women, steal, fight, and spoil for their mistresses' sakes.
And no king so strong, but a fair woman is stronger than
he is. All things' (as he proceeds) 'fear to touch the king;
yet I saw him and Apame his concubine, the daughter
of the famous Bartacus, sitting on the right hand of the
king, and she took the crown off his head, and put it on

her own, and stroke him with her left hand; yet the king gaped and gazed on her, and when she laughed he laughed, and when she was angry he flattered to be reconciled to her.' So beauty commands even kings themselves; nay, whole armies and kingdoms are captivated together with their kings. *Forma vincit armatos, ferrum pulchritudo captivat; vincentur specie, qui non vincentur prælio* [beauty conquers warriors, grace overcomes the sword; they will be subdued by beauty who are not subdued in battle]. And 'tis a great matter, saith Xenophon, 'and of which all fair persons may worthily brag, that a strong man must labour for his living if he will have aught, a valiant man must fight and endanger himself for it, a wise man speak, show himself, and toil; but a fair and beautiful person doth all with ease, he compasseth his desire without any painstaking': God and men, heaven and earth conspire to honour him; every one pities him above other, if he be in need, and all the world is willing to do him good. Chariclea fell into the hand of pirates, but when all the rest were put to the edge of the sword, she alone was preserved for her person. When Constantinople was sacked by the Turk, Irene escaped, and was so far from being made a captive, that she even captivated the Grand Seignior himself. So did Rosamond insult over King Henry the Second:

> I was so fair an object;
> Whom fortune made my king, my love made subject;
> He found by proof the privilege of beauty,
> That it had power to countermand all duty.

It captivates the very gods themselves, *morosiora numina* [the more austere deities]:

> *Deus ipse deorum*
> *Factus ob hanc formam bos, equus, imber, olor.*

[The king of the gods for the sake of this beauty made himself a bull, a horse, a shower, a swan.]

And those *mali genii* [evil spirits] are taken with it, as I have already proved. *Formosam barbari verentur, et ad aspectum pulchrum immanis animus mansuescit* (Heliodorus, *lib.* 5): the barbarians stand in awe of a fair woman, and at a beautiful aspect a fierce spirit is pacified. For whenas Troy was taken, and the wars ended (as Clemens Alexandrinus quotes out of Euripides), angry Menelaus, with rage and fury armed, came with his sword drawn, to have killed Helena with his own hands, as being the sole cause of all those wars and miseries; but when he saw her fair face, as one amazed at her divine beauty, he let his weapon fall, and embraced her besides; he had no power to strike so sweet a creature. *Ergo hebetantur enses pulchritudine*, the edge of a sharp sword (as the saying is) is dulled with a beautiful aspect, and severity itself is overcome. Hyperides the orator, when Phryne his client was accused at Athens for her lewdness, used no other defence in her cause, but tearing her upper garment, disclosed her naked breast to the judges, with which comeliness of her body and amiable gesture they were so moved and astonished that they did acquit her forthwith, and let her go. O noble piece of justice! mine author exclaims: and who is he that would not rather lose his seat and robes, forfeit his office, than give sentence against the majesty of beauty? Such prerogatives have fair persons, and they alone are free from danger. Parthenopæus was so lovely and fair, that when he fought in the Theban wars, if his face had been by chance bare, no enemy would offer to strike at or hurt him, such immunities hath beauty. Beasts themselves are moved with it. Sinalda was a woman of such excellent feature, and a queen, that when she was to be trodden on by wild horses for a punishment, 'the wild beasts stood in admiration of her person' (Saxo Grammaticus, *lib*. 8 *Dan. Hist*.) 'and would not hurt her.' Wherefore did that royal virgin in Apuleius, when she fled from the thieves' den, in a desert, make such an apostrophe to her ass on whom she rode (for what knew she to the contrary, but that he was an ass?): *Si me parentibus et proco formoso reddideris, quas tibi gratias, quos honores habebo, quos cibos exhibebo?* [If you take me back to my parents and my fair betrothed I shall be grateful to you and honour you without end, I shall give you the finest food.] She would comb him, dress him, feed him, and trick him every day herself, and he should work no more, toil no more, but rest and play, etc. And besides, she would have a dainty picture drawn, in perpetual remembrance, a virgin riding upon an ass's back, with this motto, *Asino vectore regia virgo fugiens captivitatem* [a royal maid riding upon an ass to escape captivity]. Why said she all this? why did she make such promises to a dumb beast? but that she perceived the poor ass to be taken with her beauty; for he did often *obliquo collo pedes puellæ decoros basiare*, kiss her feet as she rode, *et ad delicatulas voculas tentabat adhinnire*, offer to give consent as much as in him was to her delicate speeches, and besides he had some feeling, as she conceived, of her misery. And why did Theagines' horse in Heliodorus curvet, prance, and go so proudly, *exultans alacriter et superbiens*, etc., but that sure, as mine author supposeth, he was in love with his master? *dixisses ipsum equum pulchrum intelligere pulchram domini formam* [you would have said that the horse itself was aware of the beauty of its master]. A fly lighted on Malthius' cheek as he lay asleep: but why? Not to hurt him, as a parasite of his, standing by, well perceived, *non ut pungeret, sed ut oscularetur*, but certainly to kiss him, as ravished with his divine looks. Inanimate creatures, I suppose, have a touch of this. When a drop of Psyche's candle fell on Cupid's shoulder, I think sure it was to kiss it. When Venus ran to meet her rose-cheeked Adonis, as an elegant poet of ours sets her out,

> The bushes in the way
> Some catch her neck, some kiss her face,
> Some twine about her legs to make her stay,
> And all did covet her for to embrace.

Aer ipse amore inficitur, as Heliodorus holds, the air itself is in love: for when Hero played upon her lute,

> The wanton air in twenty sweet forms danc't
> After her fingers,

and those lascivious winds stayed Daphne when she fled from Apollo:

> *Nudabant corpora venti,*
> *Obviaque adversas vibrabant flamina vestes.*

[The wind exposed her limbs as her garments fluttered in the breeze.]

Boreas ventus [the North Wind] loved Hyacinthus, and Orithyia, Erectheus' daughter of Athens: *vi rapuit*, etc., he took her away by force, as she was playing with other wenches at Ilissus, and begat Zetes and Calais his two sons of her. That seas and waters are enamoured with this our beauty, is all out as likely as that of the air and winds; for when Leander swimmed in the Hellespont, Neptune with his trident did beat down the waves, but they

> Still mounted up, intending to have kissed him,
> And fell in drops like tears because they missed him.

The river Alpheus was in love with Arethusa, as she tells the tale herself:

> *Viridesque manu siccata capillos,*
> *Fluminis Alphei veteres recitavit amores:*
> *Pars ego Nympharum, etc.*

[As with her hand she wiped the moisture from her green tresses, she thus recounted the bygone love of the stream Alpheus. 'I was once a nymph,' etc.]

When our Thame and Isis meet,

> *Oscula mille sonant, connexu brachia pallent,*
> *Mutuaque explicitis connectunt colla lacertis.*

> [They exchanged a thousand kisses, and with
> arms intertwined hang on each other's neck.]

Inachus and Peneus, and how many loving rivers can I
reckon up, whom beauty hath enthralled! I say nothing
all this while of idols themselves that have committed
idolatry in this kind, of looking-glasses that have been
rapt in love (if you will believe poets), when their ladies
and mistresses looked on to dress them.

> *Et si non habeo sensum, tua gratia sensum*
>   *Exhibet, et calidi sentio amoris onus.*
> *Dirigis huc quoties spectantia lumina, flamma*
>   *Succendunt inopi saucia membra mihi.*

> Though I no sense at all of feeling have,
> Yet your sweet looks do animate and save;
> And when your speaking eyes do this way turn,
> Methinks my wounded members live and burn.

I could tell you such another story of a spindle that was
fired by a fair lady's looks, or fingers, some say, I know
not well whether, but fired it was by report, and of a
cold bath that suddenly smoked and was very hot when
naked Cælia came into it: *Miramur quis sit tantus et unde
vapor* [we marvel whence comes this great steam],

etc. But of all the tales in this kind, that is the most memorable of Death himself, when he should have stroken a sweet young virgin with his dart, he fell in love with the object. Many more such could I relate which are to be believed with a poetical faith. So dumb and dead creatures dote, but men are mad, stupefied many times at the first sight of beauty, amazed, as that fisherman in Aristænetus, that spied a maid bathing herself by the sea-side:

Soluta mihi sunt omnia membra
A capite ad calcem, sensusque omnis periit
De pectore, tam immensus stupor animam invasit mihi.

[My limbs quivered, I shook from head to foot, my senses left me, I was utterly dazed and stupefied.]

And as Lucian, in his Images, confesses of himself, that he was at his mistress's presence void of all sense, immovable, as if he had seen a Gorgon's head: which was no such cruel monster (as Cælius interprets it, *lib.* 3, *cap.* 9), 'but the very quintessence of beauty,' some fair creature, as without doubt the poet understood in the first fiction of it, at which the spectators were amazed. *Miseri quibus intentata nites,* poor wretches are compelled at the very sight of her ravishing looks to run mad, or make away themselves.

> They wait the sentence of her scornful eyes;
> And whom she favours lives, the other dies.

Heliodorus, *lib.* I, brings in Thyamis almost besides himself, when he saw Chariclea first, and not daring to look upon her a second time, 'for he thought it unpossible for any man living to see her and contain himself.' The very fame of beauty will fetch them to it many miles off (such an attractive power this loadstone hath), and they will seem but short, they will undertake any toil or trouble, long journeys, Penia or Atalanta shall not overgo them, through seas, deserts, mountains, and dangerous places, as they did to gaze on Psyche: 'many mortal men came far and near to see that glorious object of her age'; Paris for Helena, Corebus to Troy,

> *Illis Trojam qui forte diebus*
> *Venerat insano Cassandræ incensus amore.*

[Who chanced to have then arrived in Troy, drawn by his burning passion for Cassandra.]

King John of France, once prisoner in England, came to visit his old friends again, crossing the seas; but the truth is, his coming was to see the Countess of Salisbury, the nonpareil of those times, and his dear mistress. That infernal god Plutus came from hell itself, to steal Proserpina; Achilles left all his friends for Polyxena's sake, his enemy's daughter; and all the Grecian gods forsook their heavenly mansions for that fair lady, Philo Dioneus' daughter's sake, the paragon of Greece in those days; *ea enim venustate fuit, ut eam certatim omnes dii conjugem expeterent* [for she was of such surpassing beauty that all the gods contended for her love]: *Formosa divis imperat puella* [the beautiful maid commands the gods]. They will not only come to see, but as a falconer makes an hungry hawk, hover about, follow, give attendance and service, spend goods, lives, and all their fortunes to attain:

> Were beauty under twenty locks kept fast,
> Yet love breaks through, and picks them all at last.

When fair Hero came abroad, the eyes, hearts, and affections of her spectators were still attendant on her.

> *Et medios inter vultus supereminet omnes,*
> *Perque urbem aspiciunt venientem numinis instar.*

> So far above the rest fair Hero shined,
> And stole away the enchanted gazer's mind.

When Peter Aretine's Lucretia came first to Rome, and that the fame of her beauty *ad urbanarum deliciarum sectatores venerat, nemo non ad videndam eam*, etc., was spread abroad, they came in (as they say) 'thick and threefold' to see her, and hovered about her gates, as they did of old to Lais of Corinth, and Phryne of Thebes, *Ad cujus jacuit Græcia tota fores* [at whose gates lay all Greece]. 'Every man sought to get her love, some with gallant and costly apparel, some with an affected pace, some with music, others with rich gifts, pleasant discourse, multitude of followers; others with letters, vows, and promises, to commend themselves, and to be gracious in her eyes.' Happy was he that could see her, thrice happy that enjoyed her company. Charmides in Plato was a proper young man, in comeliness of person, 'and all good qualities, far exceeding others; whensoever fair Charmides came abroad, they seemed all to be in love with him' (as Critias describes their carriage), 'and were troubled at the very sight of him; many came near him, many followed him wheresoever he went,' as those *formarum spectatores* [who were looking out for beauties] did Acontius, if at any time he walked abroad: the Athenian lasses stared on Alcibiades; Sappho and the Mitylenian women on Phaon the fair. Such lovely sights do not only please, entice, but ravish and amaze. Cleonymus, a delicate and tender youth, present at a feast which Androcles his uncle made *in Piræo* [in the Piræus] at Athens, when he sacrificed to Mercury, so stupefied the guests, Dineas, Aristippus, Agasthenes, and the rest (as Charidemus in Lucian relates it), that they could not eat their meat, they sat all supper-time gazing, glancing at him, stealing looks, and admiring of his beauty. Many will condemn these men that are so enamoured for fools; but some again commend them for it; many reject Paris' judgment, and yet Lucian approves of it, admiring Paris for his choice; he would have done as much himself, and by good desert in his mind; beauty is to be preferred 'before wealth or wisdom.' Athenæus, *Deipnosophist. lib.* 13, *cap.* 7, holds it not such indignity for the Trojans and Greeks to contend ten years, to spend so much labour, lose so many men's lives for Helen's sake, for so fair a lady's sake:

Ob talem uxorem cui præstantissima forma,
Nil mortale refert.

[Compared with a woman of such peerless beauty,
nothing human matters.]

That one woman was worth a kingdom, an hundred thousand other women, a world itself. Well might Stesichorus be blind for carping at so fair a creature, and a just punishment it was. The same testimony gives Homer of the old men of Troy, that were spectators of that single combat between Paris and Menelaus at the Scæan gate, when Helena stood in presence; they said all, the war was worthily prolonged and undertaken for her sake. The very gods themselves (as Homer and Isocrates record) fought more for Helena than they did against the giants. When Venus lost her son Cupid, she made proclamation by Mercury, that he that could bring tidings of him should have seven kisses; a noble reward some say, and much better than so many golden talents; seven such kisses to many men were more precious than seven cities, or so many provinces. One such a kiss alone would recover a man if he were a-dying: *Suaviolum Stygia sic te de valle reducet*, etc. Great Alexander married Roxane, a poor man's child, only for her person. 'Twas well done of Alexander, and heroically done; I admire him for it. Orlando was mad for Angelica, and who doth not condole his mishap? Thisbe died for Pyramus, Dido for Æneas; who doth not weep, as (before his conversion) Austin did, in commiseration of her estate? she died for him; 'methinks' (as he said) 'I could die for her.'

But this is not the matter in hand; what prerogative this beauty hath, of what power and sovereignty it is, and how far such persons that so much admire and dote upon it are to be justified – no man doubts of these matters; the question is, how and by what means beauty produceth this effect? By sight: the eye betrays the soul, and is both active and passive in this business; it wounds and is wounded, is an especial cause and instrument, both in the subject and in the object. 'As tears, it begins in the eyes, descends to the breast'; it conveys these beauteous rays, as I have said, unto the heart. *Ut vidi, ut perii!* [I saw, I was undone]. *Mars videt hanc, visamque cupit* [Mars sees her and straightway desires her]. Shechem saw Dinah the daughter of Leah, and defiled her (Gen. xxxiv, 3); Jacob, Rachel (xxix, 17), 'for she was beautiful and fair'; David spied Bathsheba afar off (2 Sam. xi, 2); the Elders, Susanna, as that Orthomenian Strato saw fair Aristoclea, the daughter of Theophanes, bathing herself at that Hercyne well in Lebadea, and were captivated in an instant. *Viderunt oculi, rapuerunt pectora flammæ* [the eyes beheld, the heart was straight aflame]. Amnon fell sick for Tamar's sake (2 Sam. xiii, 2). The beauty of Esther was such, that she found favour not only in the sight of Ahasuerus, 'but of all those that looked upon her.' Gerson, Origen, and some others contended that Christ Himself was the fairest of the sons of men, and Joseph next unto Him, *speciosus præ filiis hominum*, and they will have it literally taken; His very person was such that He found grace and favour of all those that looked upon Him. Joseph was so fair, that, as the ordinary gloss hath it, *filiæ decurrerent per murum, et ad fenestras*, they ran to the top of the walls and to the windows to gaze on him, as we do commonly to see some great personage go by: and so Matthew Paris describes Matilda the Empress going through Cologne. P. Morales the Jesuit saith as much of the Virgin Mary. Antony no sooner saw Cleopatra, but, saith Appian, *lib.* I, he was enamoured of her. Theseus at the first sight of Helen was so besotted, that he esteemed himself the happiest man in the world if he might enjoy her, and to that purpose kneeled down, and made his pathetical prayers unto the gods. Charicles, by chance espying that curious picture of smiling Venus naked in her temple, stood a great while gazing, as one amazed; at length he brake into that mad passionate speech, 'O fortunate god Mars, that wast bound in chains, and made ridiculous for her sake!' He could not contain himself, but kissed her picture, I know not how oft, and heartily desired to be so disgraced as Mars was. And what did he that his betters had not done before him?

> *Atque aliquis de dis non tristibus optat*
> *Sic fieri turpis.*

When Venus came first to heaven, her comeliness was such, that (as mine author saith) 'all the gods came flocking about, and saluted her, each of them went to Jupiter, and desired he might have her to be his wife.' When fair Autolycus came in presence, as a candle in the dark his beauty shined, all men's eyes (as Xenophon describes the manner of it) 'were instantly fixed on him, and moved at the sight, insomuch that they could not

conceal themselves, but in gesture or looks it was discerned and expressed.' Those other senses, hearing,
touching, may much penetrate and affect, but none so
much, none so forcible as sight. *Forma Briseis mediis in
armis movit Achillem*, Achilles was moved in the midst of
a battle by fair Briseis, Ajax by Tecmessa; Judith captivated that great captain Holofernes: Delilah, Samson;
Rosamund, Henry the Second; Roxalana, Solyman the
Magnificent, etc.

> Νικᾶ δὲ καὶ σιδηρον
> Καὶ πῦρ καλή τις ουσα.

A fair woman overcomes fire and sword.

> Naught under heaven so strongly doth allure
> The sense of man and all his mind possess,
> As beauty's loveliest bait, that doth procure
> Great warriors erst their rigour to suppress,
> And mighty hands forget their manliness,
> Driven with the power of an heart-burning eye,
> And lapt in fetters of a golden tress,
> That can with melting pleasure mollify
> Their harden'd hearts inur'd to cruelty.

Clitiphon ingenuously confesseth, that he no sooner
came in Leucippe's presence, but that he did *corde tremere,
et oculis lascivius intueri*; he was wounded at the first
sight, his heart panted, and he could not possibly turn
his eyes from her. So doth Calasiris in Heliodorus, *lib.* 2,
Isis' priest, a reverend old man, complain, who by chance

at Memphis seeing that Thracian Rhodopis, might not hold his eyes off her: 'I will not conceal it, she overcame me with her presence, and quite assaulted my continency which I had kept unto mine old age; I resisted a long time my bodily eyes with the eyes of my understanding; at last I was conquered, and as in a tempest carried headlong.' Xenopithes, a philosopher, railed at women downright for many years together, scorned, hated, scoffed at them; coming at last into Daphnis a fair maid's company (as he condoles his mishap to his friend Demaretus), though free before, *contactus nullis ante cupidinibus*, was far in love, and quite overcome upon a sudden. *Victus sum, fateor, a Daphnide*, etc., I confess I am taken,

> *Sola hæc inflexit sensus, animumque labentem*
> *Impulit,*

[She alone hath made me waver and turned my mind,]

I could hold out no longer. Such another mishap, but worse, had Stratocles the physician, that blear-eyed old man, *muco plenus* (so Prodromus describes him); he was a severe woman-hater all his life, *fæda et contumeliosa semper in feminas profatus*, a bitter persecutor of the whole sex, *humanas aspides et viperas appellabat* [he called them asps and vipers in human shape], he forswore them all still, and mocked them wheresoever he came, in such vile terms, *ut matrem et sorores odisses*, that if thou hadst heard him, thou wouldst have loathed thine own mother and sisters for his word's sake. Yet this old doting fool was taken at last with that celestial and divine look of Myrilla, the daughter of Anticles the gardener, that smirking wench, that he shaved off his bushy beard, painted his face, curled his hair, wore a laurel crown to cover his bald pate, and for her love besides was ready to run mad. For the very day that he married he was so furious, *ut solis occasum minus expectare posset* (a terrible, a monstrous long day), he could not stay till it was night, *sed omnibus insalutatis in thalamum festinans irrupit*, the meat scarce out of his mouth, without any leave-taking, he would needs go presently to bed. What young man, therefore, if old men be so intemperate, can secure himself? Who can say, I will not be taken with a beautiful object, I can, I will contain? No, saith Lucian of his mistress, she is so fair, that if thou dost but see her, 'she will stupefy thee, kill thee straight, and, Medusa-like, turn thee to a stone; thou canst not pull thine eyes from her, but, as an adamant doth iron, she will carry thee bound headlong whither she will herself,' infect thee like a basilisk. It holds both in men and women. Dido was amazed at Æneas' presence: *Obstupuit primo aspectu Sidonia Dido*; and, as he feelingly verified out of his experience:

> *Quam ego postquam vidi, non ita amavi ut sani solent*
> *Homines, sed eodem pacto ut insani solent.*

> I lov'd her not as others soberly,
> But as a madman rageth, so did I.

So Musæus of Leander, *nusquam lumen detorquet ab illa* [he never turned his eyes from her]; and Chaucer of Palamon,

> He cast his eye upon Emilia,
> And therewith he blent and cried ha, ha,
> As though he had been stroke unto the heart.

If you desire to know more particularly what this beauty is, how it doth *influere* [influence], how it doth fascinate (for, as all hold, love is a fascination), thus in brief. 'This comeliness or beauty ariseth from the due proportion of the whole, or from each several part.' For an exact delineation of which, I refer you to poets, historiographers, and those amorous writers, to Lucian's *Imagines* and *Charidemus*, Xenophon's description of Panthea, Petronius' *Catalecta*, Heliodorus' Chariclea, Tatius' Leucippe, Longus Sophista's Daphnis and Chloe, Theodorus Prodromus his Rhodanthe, Aristænetus' and Philostratus' Epistles, Balthasar Castilio, *lib. 4 de aulico*, Laurentius, *cap.* 10 *de melan.*, Æneas Sylvius his Lucretia, and every poet almost, which have most accurately described a perfect beauty, an absolute feature, and that through every member, both in men and women. Each part must concur to the perfection of it; for as Seneca saith, *Ep. 33, lib. 4, Non est formosa mulier cujus crus laudatur et brachium, sed illa cujus simul universa facies admirationem singulis partibus dedit:* she is no fair woman, whose arm, thigh, etc., are commended, except the face and all the other parts be correspondent. And the face especially gives a lustre to the rest: the face is it that commonly denominates fair or foul: *arx formæ facies*, the face is beauty's tower; and though the other parts be deformed, yet a good face carries it (*facies non uxor amatur* ['tis the face, not the wife, that is loved]), that alone is most part respected, principally valued, *deliciis suis ferox*, and of itself able to captivate.

> *Urit te Glyceræ nitor,*
> *Urit grata protervitas*
> *Et vultus nimium lubricus aspici.*

Glycera's too fair a face was it that set him on fire, too fine to be beheld. When Chærea saw the singing-wench's sweet looks, he was so taken, that he cried out, *O faciem pulchram, deleo omnes dehinc ex animo mulieres, tædet quotidianarum harum formarum!* 'O fair face, I'll never love any but her, look on any other hereafter but her; I am weary of these ordinary beauties, away with them!' The more he sees her, the worse he is, *uritque videndo*; as in a burning-glass the sunbeams are re-collected to a centre, the rays of love are projected from her eyes. It was Æneas' countenance ravished Queen Dido, *os humerosque deo similis*, he had an angelical face.

> *O sacros vultus Baccho vel Apolline dignos,*
> *Quos vir, quos tuto femina nulla videt!*

> O sacred looks, befitting majesty,
> Which never mortal wight could safely see!

Although for the greater part this beauty be most emi-nent in the face, yet many times those other members yield a most pleasing grace, and are alone sufficient to enamour. An high brow like unto the bright heavens, *Cœli pulcherrima plaga, Frons ubi vivit honor, frons ubi ludit amor* [a brow where honour dwells and love disports], white and smooth like the polished alabaster, a pair of cheeks of vermilion colour, in which love lodgeth: *Amor qui mollibus genis puellæ pernoctas* [love that dallies on a maid's soft cheeks]; a coral lip, *suaviorum delubrum* [a shrine of kisses], in which *Basia mille patent, basia mille latent* [a thousand kisses show, a thousand lie hid], *gratiarum sedes gratissima* [sweetest abode of sweetness]; a sweet-smelling flower, from which bees may gather honey:

> *Mellilegæ volucres, quid adhuc cava thyma rosasque, etc.*
>> *Omnes ad dominæ labra venite meæ,*
> *Illa rosas spirat, etc.*

[Ye honey-gathering bees, wherefore seek ye thyme and roses? Come all to the lips of my mistress, she breathes roses, etc.]

A white and round neck, that *via lactea* [milky way]; dimple in the chin, black eyebrows, *Cupidinis arcus* [Cupid's bow], sweet breath, white and even teeth; [that] which some call the sale-piece, a fine soft round pap, gives an excellent grace, *Quale decus tumidis Pario de marmore mammis!* and make a pleasant valley, *lacteum sinum*, between two chalky hills, *sororiantes papillulas, et ad pruritum frigidos amatores solo aspectu excitantes. Unde is, Forma papillarum quam fuit apta premi!* – Again, *Urebant oculos duræ stantesque mamillæ.*

A flaxen hair: golden hair was even in great account, for which Virgil commends Dido, *Nondum sustulerat flavum Proserpinina crinem* [not yet had Proserpine put up her golden hair], *Et crines nodantur in aurum* [the hair is tied in a golden knot]. Apollonius (*Argonaut. lib. 4, Jasonis flava coma incendit cor Medeæ*) will have Jason's golden hair to be the main cause of Medea's dotage on him. Castor and Pollux were both yellow-haired; Paris, Menelaus, and most amorous young men have been such in all ages, *molles ac suaves*, as Baptista Porta infers, *Physiog. lib. 2*, lovely to behold. Homer so commends Helen, makes Patroclus and Achilles both yellow-haired; *pulchricoma* [fair-haired] Venus; and Cupid himself was yellow-haired, *in aurum coruscante et crispante capillo* [with bright curly golden locks], like that neat picture of Narcissus in Callistratus, for so Psyche spied him asleep; Briseis, Polyxena, etc., *flavicomæ omnes* [were all yellow-haired],

> And Hero the fair,
> Whom young Apollo courted for her hair.

Leland commends Guithera, King Arthur's wife, for a fair flaxen hair: so Paulus Æmilius sets out Clodoveus, that lovely king of France. Synesius holds every effeminate fellow or adulterer is fair-haired: and Apuleius adds that Venus herself, Goddess of Love, cannot delight, 'though she come accompanied with the Graces, and all Cupid's train to attend upon her, girt with her own girdle, and smell of cinnamon and balm, yet if she be bald or bad-haired, she cannot please her Vulcan.' Which belike makes our Venetian ladies at this day to counterfeit yellow hair so much, great women to calamistrate and curl it up, *vibrantes ad gratiam crines, et tot orbibus in captivitatem flexos*, to adorn their heads with spangles, pearls, and made flowers; and all courtiers to affect a pleasing grace in this kind. In a word, 'the hairs are Cupid's nets, to catch all comers, a brushy wood, in which Cupid builds his nest, and under whose shadow all loves a thousand several ways sport themselves.'

A little soft hand, pretty little mouth, small, fine long fingers (*Gratia quæ digitis*, 'tis that which Apollo did admire in Daphne: *laudat digitosque manusque*), a straight and slender body, a small foot, and well-proportioned leg hath an excellent lustre, *cui totum incumbit corpus uti fundamento ædes* [on which the whole body rests as a house on its foundation]. Clearchus vowed to his friend Amynander in Aristænetus, that the most attractive part in his mistress, to make him love and like her first, was her pretty leg and foot: a soft and white skin, etc., have their peculiar graces: *Nebula haud est mollior ac hujus cutis est, edepol papillam bellulam* [a cloud cannot be softer than this maid's skin; a pretty little pap, forsooth]. Though in men these parts are not so much respected; a grim Saracen sometimes, *nudus membra Pyracmon* [a bare-limbed Cyclops], a martial hirsute face pleaseth best; a black man is a pearl in a fair woman's eye, and is as acceptable as lame Vulcan was to Venus; for he, being a sweaty fuliginous blacksmith, was dearly beloved of her, when fair Apollo, nimble Mercury were rejected, and the rest of the sweet-faced gods forsaken. Many women (as Petronius observes) *sordibus calent* [fall in love with low fellows] (as many men are more moved with kitchen-wenches, and a poor market-maid, than all these

illustrious court and city dames), will sooner dote upon
a slave, a servant, a dirt-dauber, a Brontes, a cook, a
player, if they see his naked legs or arms, *torosaque brachia*
[brawny arms], etc., like that huntsman Meleager in
Philostratus, though he be all in rags, obscene and dirty,
besmeared like a ruddle-man, a gipsy, or a chimney-
sweeper, than upon a noble gallant, Nireus, Hephæstion,
Alcibiades, or those embroidered courtiers full of silk
and gold. Justin's wife, a citizen of Rome, fell in love
with Pylades a player, and was ready to run mad for him,
had not Galen himself helped her by chance. Faustina the
empress doted on a fencer.

Not one of a thousand falls in love, but there is some
peculiar part or other which pleaseth most, and inflames
him above the rest. A company of young philosophers
on a time fell at variance, which part of a woman was
most desirable and pleased best? some said the forehead,
some the teeth, some the eyes, cheeks, lips, neck, chin,
etc.; the controversy was referred to Lais of Corinth to
decide; but she, smiling, said they were a company of
fools; for suppose they had her where they wished, what
would they first seek? Yet, this notwithstanding, I do
easily grant, *neque quis vestrum negaverit, opinor* [and none
of you, I think, will gainsay it], all parts are attractive,
but especially the eyes,

> *Videt igne micantes,*
> *Sideribus similes oculos,*

[He sees her eyes sparkling like the stars,]

which are love's fowlers, *aucupium amoris*; the shoeing-horns, 'the hooks of love' (as Arandus will), 'the guides, touchstone, judges, that in a moment cure madmen and make sound folks mad, the watchmen of the body; what do they not? how vex they not?' All this is true, and (which Athenæus, *lib.* 13 *Deipnosoph. cap.* 5, and Tatius hold) they are the chief seats of love, and as James Lernutius hath facetely expressed in an elegant ode of his:

> *Amorem ocellis flammeolis heræ*
> *Vidi insidentem, credite posteri,*
> *Fratresque circum ludibundos*
> *Cum pharetra volitare et arcu*, etc.

> I saw Love sitting in my mistress' eyes
>   Sparkling, believe it all posterity,
> And his attendants playing round about
>   With bow and arrows ready for to fly.

Scaliger calls the eyes 'Cupid's arrows; the tongue, the lightning of love; the paps, the tents': Balthasar Castilio, the causes, the chariots, the lamps of love:

> *Æmula lumina stellis,*
> *Lumina quæ possent sollicitare deos;*

> Eyes emulating stars in light,
>   Enticing gods at the first sight;

Love's orators, Petronius:

O blandos oculos, et o facetos,
Et quadam propria nota loquaces:
Illic est Venus, et leves amores,
Atque ipsa in medio sedet voluptas;

O sweet and pretty speaking eyes,
Where Venus, love, and pleasure lies;

Love's torches, touch-box, naphtha, and matches, Tibullus:

Illius ex oculis quum vult exurere divos,
Accendit geminas lampadas acer amor.

Tart Love, when he will set the gods on fire,
Lightens the eyes as torches to desire.

Leander, at the first sight of Hero's eyes, was incensed, saith Musæus:

Simul in oculorum radiis crescebat fax amorum,
Et cor fervebat invecti ignis impetu;
Pulchritudo enim celebris immaculatæ feminæ,
Acutior hominibus est veloci sagitta.
Oculus vero via est, ab oculi ictibus
Vulnus dilabitur, et in præcordia viri manat.

Love's torches 'gan to burn first in her eyes,
And set his heart on fire which never dies:
For the fair beauty of a virgin pure
Is sharper than a dart, and doth inure

A deeper wound, which pierceth to the heart
By the eyes, and causeth such a cruel smart.

A modern poet brings in Amnon complaining of Tamar:

> *Et me fascino*
> *Occidit ille risus et formæ lepos,*
> *Ille nitor, illa gratia, et verus decor,*
> *Illæ æmulantes purpuram, et rosas genæ,*
> *Oculique vinctæque aureo nodo comæ.*

> It was thy beauty, 'twas thy pleasing smile,
> Thy grace and comeliness did me beguile;
> Thy rose-like cheeks and unto purple fair,
> Thy lovely eyes and golden knotted hair.

Philostratus Lemnius cries out on his mistress' basilisk eyes, *ardentes faces*, those two burning-glasses, they had so inflamed his soul, that no water could quench it. 'What a tyranny' (saith he), 'what a penetration of bodies is this! thou drawest with violence, and swallowest me up, as Charybdis doth sailors, with thy rocky eyes: he that falls into this gulf of love can never get out.' Let this be the corollary then, the strongest beams of beauty are still darted from the eyes.

> *Nam quis lumina tanta, tanta*
> *Posset luminibus suis tueri,*
> *Non statim trepidansque, palpitansque,*
> *Præ desiderii æstuantis aura?* etc.

> For who such eyes with his can see,
> And not forthwith enamoured be!

And as men catch dotterels by putting out a leg or an arm, with those mutual glances of the eyes they first inveigle one another. *Cynthia prima suis miserum me cepit ocellis* ['twas with her eyes that Cynthia first led me captive]. Of all eyes (by the way) black are most amiable, enticing and fairest, which the poet observes in commending of his mistress, *Spectandum nigris oculis, nigroque capillo* [notable for black eyes and black hair], which Hesiod admires in his Alcmena,

> *Cujus a vertice ac nigricantibus oculis,*
> *Tale quiddam spirat ac ab aurea Venere.*

> From her black eyes, and from her golden face,
> As if from Venus came a lovely grace

and Triton in his Milane, *Nigra oculos formosa mihi* [a black-eyed maid to me is beautiful]. Homer useth that epithet of ox-eyed in describing Juno, because a round black eye is the best, the son of beauty, and farthest from black the worse; which Polydore Virgil taxeth in our nation: *Angli ut plurimum cæsiis oculis*, we have grey eyes for the most part. Baptista Porta, *Physiognom. lib.* 3, puts grey colour upon children, they be childish eyes, dull and heavy. Many commend on the other side Spanish ladies, and those Greek dames at this day, for the blackness of their eyes, as Porta doth his Neapolitan young wives. Suetonius describes Julius Cæsar to have been

nigris vegetisque oculis micantibus, of a black quick sparkling eye: and although Averroes, in his *Colliget*, will have
such persons timorous, yet without question they are
most amorous.

Now, last of all, I will show you by what means beauty
doth fascinate, bewitch, as some hold, and work upon
the soul of a man by the eye. For certainly I am of the
poet's mind, love doth bewitch and strangely change us.

> *Ludit amor sensus, oculos perstringit, et aufert*
> *Libertatem animi, mira nos fascinat arte.*
> *Credo aliquis dæmon subiens præcordia flammam*
> *Concitat, et raptam tollit de cardine mentem.*

> Love mocks our senses, curbs our liberties,
> And doth bewitch us with his art and rings,
> I think some devil gets into our entrails,
> And kindles coals, and heaves our souls from th' hinges.

Heliodorus, *lib.* 3, proves at large that love is witchcraft,
'it gets in at our eyes, pores, nostrils, engenders the same
qualities and affections in us, as were in the party whence
it came.' The manner of the fascination, as Ficinus, 10
cap. Com. in Plat., declares it, is thus: 'Mortal men are
then especially bewitched, whenas by often gazing one
on the other they direct sight to sight, join eye to eye,
and so drink and suck in love between them; for the
beginning of this disease is the eye. And therefore he
that hath a clear eye, though he be otherwise deformed,
by often looking upon him, will make one mad, and tie
him fast to him by the eye.' Leonard. Varius, *lib.* 1, *cap.*

2, *de fascinat.*, telleth us that by this interview 'the purer spirits are infected,' the one eye pierceth through the other with his rays, which he sends forth, and many men have those excellent piercing eyes, that, which Suetonius relates of Augustus, their brightness is such, they compel their spectators to look off, and can no more endure them than the sunbeams. Barradius, *lib. 6, cap.* 10, *de Harmonia Evangel.*, reports as much of our Saviour Christ, and Peter Morales of the Virgin Mary, whom Nicephorus describes likewise to have been yellow-haired, of a wheat colour, but of a most amiable and piercing eye. The rays, as some think, sent from the eyes, carry certain spiritual vapours with them, and so infect the other party, and that in a moment. I know, they that hold *visio fit intra mittendo* [sight comes from receiving the images] will make a doubt of this; but Ficinus proves it from blear-eyes, 'that by sight alone make others blear-eyed; and it is more than manifest that the vapour of the corrupt blood doth get in together with the rays, and so by the contagion the spectator's eyes are infected.' Other arguments there are of a basilisk, that kills afar off by sight, as that Ephesian did of whom Philostratus speaks, of so pernicious an eye, he poisoned all he looked steadily on: and that other argument, *menstruæ feminæ*, out of Aristotle's Problems, *morbosæ* Capivaccius adds, and Septalius the Commentator, that contaminate a looking-glass with beholding it. 'So the beams that come from the agent's heart, by the eyes, infect the spirits about the patients, inwardly wound, and thence the spirits infect the blood.' To this effect she complained in Apuleius, 'Thou art the cause of my grief; thy eyes, piercing through mine eyes to mine inner parts, have set my bowels on fire, and therefore pity me that am now ready to die for thy sake.' Ficinus illustrates this with a familiar example of that Marrhusian Phædrus and Theban Lycias: 'Lycias he stares on Phædrus' face, and Phædrus fastens the balls of his eyes upon Lycias, and with those sparkling rays sends out his spirits. The beams of Phædrus' eyes are easily mingled with the beams of Lycias', and spirits are joined to spirits. This vapour, begot in Phædrus' heart, enters into Lycias' bowels: and that which is a greater wonder, Phædrus' blood is in Lycias' heart, and thence come those ordinary love-speeches, My sweet-heart Phædrus! and mine own self, my dear bowels! And Phædrus again to Lycias, O my light, my joy, my soul, my life! Phædrus follows Lycias, because his heart would have his spirits; and Lycias follows Phædrus, because he loves the seat of his spirits; both follow, but Lycias the earnester of the two: the river hath more need of the fountain than the fountain of the river; as iron is drawn to that which is touched with a loadstone, but draws not it again, so Lycias draws Phædrus.' But how comes it to pass, then, that a blind man loves, that never saw? We read, in the Lives of the Fathers, a story of a child that was brought up in the wilderness, from his infancy, by an old hermit: now come to man's estate, he saw by chance two comely women wandering in the woods: he asked the old man what creatures they were, he told him fairies; after a while, talking *obiter* [casually], the hermit demanded of him, which was the pleasantest sight that ever he saw in his life? He readily replied, the two fairies he spied in the wilderness. So that, without doubt, there is some secret loadstone in a beautiful woman, a magnetic power, a natural inbred affection, which moves our concupiscence; and, as he sings,

> Methinks I have a mistress yet to come,
> And still I seek, I love, I know not whom.

'Tis true indeed of natural and chaste love, but not of this heroical passion, or rather brutish burning lust of which we treat; we speak of wandering, wanton, adulterous eyes, which, as he saith, 'lie still in wait as so many soldiers, and when they spy an innocent spectator fixed on them, shoot him through, and presently bewitch him: especially when they shall gaze and gloat, as wanton lovers do one upon another, and with a pleasant eye-conflict participate each other's souls.' Hence you may perceive how easily and how quickly we may be taken in love; since at the twinkling of an eye, Phædrus' spirits may so perniciously infect Lycias' blood. 'Neither is it any wonder, if we but consider how many other diseases closely, and as suddenly, are caught by infection, plague, itch, scabs, flux,' etc. The spirits, taken in, will not let him rest that hath received them, but egg him on, *idque petit corpus mens unde est saucia amore* [and the mind seeks the body whence it received its love-wound]; and we may manifestly perceive a strange eduction of spirits, by such as bleed at nose after they be dead, at the presence of the murderer; but read more of this in Lemnius, *lib.* 2 *de occult. nat. mir. cap.* 7, Valleriola, *lib.* 2 *Observ. cap.* 7, Valesius, *Controv.*, Ficinus, Cardan, Libanius *de cruentis cadaveribus*, etc.

THE STORY OF PENGUIN CLASSICS

Before 1946 ... 'Classics' are mainly the domain of academics and students; readable editions for everyone else are almost unheard of. This all changes when a little-known classicist, E. V. Rieu, presents Penguin founder Allen Lane with the translation of Homer's *Odyssey* that he has been working on in his spare time.

1946 Penguin Classics debuts with *The Odyssey*, which promptly sells three million copies. Suddenly, classics are no longer for the privileged few.

1950s Rieu, now series editor, turns to professional writers for the best modern, readable translations, including Dorothy L. Sayers's *Inferno* and Robert Graves's unexpurgated *Twelve Caesars*.

1960s The Classics are given the distinctive black covers that have remained a constant throughout the life of the series. Rieu retires in 1964, hailing the Penguin Classics list as 'the greatest educative force of the twentieth century.'

1970s A new generation of translators swells the Penguin Classics ranks, introducing readers of English to classics of world literature from more than twenty languages. The list grows to encompass more history, philosophy, science, religion and politics.

1980s The Penguin American Library launches with titles such as *Uncle Tom's Cabin*, and joins forces with Penguin Classics to provide the most comprehensive library of world literature available from any paperback publisher.

1990s The launch of Penguin Audiobooks brings the classics to a listening audience for the first time, and in 1999 the worldwide launch of the Penguin Classics website extends their reach to the global online community.

The 21st Century Penguin Classics are completely redesigned for the first time in nearly twenty years. This world-famous series now consists of more than 1300 titles, making the widest range of the best books ever written available to millions – and constantly redefining what makes a 'classic'.

The Odyssey continues ...

The best books ever written

PENGUIN  CLASSICS

SINCE 1946

Find out more at www.penguinclassics.com